"Driven by his personal work that he has taught and mastered, Ed Rose has put together a simple, yet powerful, recipe for self-fulfillment and success that is both compassionate and inspiring. Not only does the *ACTOR FACTOR* draw from a wonderfully diverse set of sources to illustrate key attributes and qualities that lie at the core of leadership and innovation, but more importantly, it provides the reader with an effective set of navigational tools for attaining a greater sense of self control and inner peace through their life journey."

—Louis A. Martin-Vega, Ph.D., P.E.
Dean of Engineering, North Carolina State University

"Ed Rose has hit another Home Run! His quick and easy to read work is thought provoking and chockfull of practical tips, memorable stories, wonderful anecdotes, and sage advice. The author has masterfully blended the enduring wisdom of societal founders like Confucius and Epictetus with the teachings of prominent business philosophers like Tom Peters and Stephen Covey, with the philosophies of Human Potential Development movement advocates like Anthony Robbins and Wayne Dyer, and with the mysticism of Buddha and Jesus, to put forth an easy-to-capture-and-apply recipe for mastering one's destiny. A definite addition to my library, it left me wanting more."

—Patrick J. Banks, Ph.D.
President/Principal Consultant, Banks International, LLC

"Ed Rose, a softball Hall of Famer, noted teacher and team builder, has finally put into words what many of us thought but couldn't convey. A practical approach to taking charge of your life instead of life taking charge of you. A thought provoking and excellent read based on over 60 years of trial and error."

—Austin O. Hollis, Jr. MAI, SRA
CEO Hollis Corporation

"I applaud your compiling the *Actor Factor*. It's important for people of all ages to read and absorb. Keep 'em active and bring out the best in others."

—**Mel Silberman, Ph.D.**
Active Training

"Ed Rose has done it again. He puts his unique, positive and practical touch on truths, which will make us all better people and team players. Ed has always been a DO IT person and the **ACTOR FACTOR** will help all readers to improve their personal performances, while increasing their contributions to others."

—**Denny Marini**
retired VP of Human Resources for Harris Semiconductor

Ed Rose's **ACTOR FACTOR** is a very engaging, on-point and thought provoking pivot piece. His ability to combine personal life experience with the enduring words of leaders and mentors we all know and trust is absolutely game-breaking. His writing style envelops the reader from the start and delivers you to a point of personal mastery…it reminds us of who we once were, asks us who we are now and drives us to become the hero of our own dreams. Ed's TOP GUN performance is a benchmark product that will serve as a literary centerpiece for many circles of warriors, leaders and winners…while maturing youth garner strength and direction from his path, aspiring professionals will be motivated by the truth of his experiences. From the combat zone to the end-zone, **ACTOR FACTOR** will take the lead role in many of my life building engagements from here on out. Thanks Ed! You continue to make us all better!

—**Anthony "Roby" Roberson, Major, USAF**
"Top-Gun" Fighter Pilot, 101 combat missions
Assistant Football Coach, US Air Force Academy Falcons

"Most people may not know this, but Ed Rose is a magician. Not just on stage, but in writing. In his *Actor Factor*, he has combined the ingredients from business experts and self-development gurus…interpreted them through the lens of his personal experiences and stories…and pulls useful tips, and sage advice, and thoughtful insights (designed to help you make sense of your life's journey from the present to the future) from these poignant pages. Quite a magic trick and very worth reading. Thanks for pulling another rabbit out of your hat."

—Harvey Robbins, Ph.D., L.P.
President, Robbins & Robbins, Inc.

Alex,
Best of luck
in life,
Ed Rose

THE ACTOR FACTOR

Are You Ready to Take the Lead Role in Your Life?

By

Ed Rose

With

Dr. Lew Losoncy

PRESS

A Division of the Diogenes Consortium

SANFORD • FLORIDA

Published by DC Press
2445 River Tree Circle
Sanford, FL 32771
http://www.focusonethics.com

For orders other than individual consumers, DC Press grants discounts on purchases of 10 or more copies of single titles for bulk use, special markets, or premium use. For further details, contact:
Special Sales — DC Press
2445 River Tree Circle, Sanford, FL 32771
TEL: 407-688-1156 • Fax: 407-688-1135
contact e-mail: contact@focusonethics.com.

Book set in Adobe Caslon
Cover Design and Composition by Jonathan Pennell

Library of Congress Catalog Number: 22008932423
        Rose. Ed,
The ACTOR Factor: Are you ready to take the lead role in your life?

        ISBN: 978-1-932021-33-2

First DC Press Edition
10   9   8   7   6   5   4   3   2   1
Printed in the United States of America

Dedication

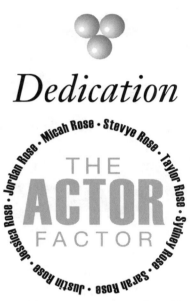

Micah Rose · Stevye Rose · Jordan Rose · Taylor Rose · Sydney Rose · Jessica Rose · Justin Rose · Sarah Rose

THE
ACTOR
FACTOR

At the time of this publication, my grandson, Justin Rose, has just received an appointment to the United States Air Force Academy. I challenge all my grandchildren to reach for their dreams.

The pride I have in my sons Edward David, Steven Phillip and Scott Michael has served to give me the incentive to put my thoughts into this book.

Remembering the words of my first true mentor, Col. Jonathan Dwight, " Life is like a cafeteria line. You get anything you want, but you have to get up and get it; no one is going to do it for you."

The world is changing at such a rapid pace, it is good to remember what Charles Darwin said, "It's not the strongest of the species that survive, nor the most intelligent, it's the ones with the ability to adapt."

Special Thanks

* * * *

In sincere appreciation for their coaching, mentoring and support during my life's journey, I want to extend a very special "thank you." With their support and encouragement I have accomplished many things I at one time could not even have imagined:

Mrs. Clark (My 5th grade teacher and "very first encourager," Carole Collins, Nancy Collins, Linda Collins, Donnie Collins, Colonel Jonathan Dwight, the Florida Air Academy, Coach Lou Houston, Jon Karl, Cheryl Rose, Alice Richmond, Bill Triggs, Ray Odom, Dr. Louis Martin-Vega, Steve Buckley, Dr. Lew Losoncy, and all my teammates over the years — too numerous to mention.

About The Authors

ED ROSE

Ed Rose is currently president of six of the nine companies he started after retiring from Harris Corporation. He has over forty years experience in industry and business from line supervision and production manager to corporate training manager to running the day-to-day operations and finances of his companies. Considered an authority on team training, experiential learning and development of Self Directed Work Teams. He is a graduate of Warner Southern College with honors in Organizational Management. Author of *Presenting and Training with Magic*, published by McGraw-Hill, *50 Ways To Teach Your Learner*, published by Jossey-Bass Pfeiffer, *The Trainer's Role in The Successful Transition To Self-Directed Work Teams*, published by American Society

Training Development. He has created numerous team-building exercises included in resource books published by McGraw-Hill and HRD Press. He has thirty-two years experience in manufacturing, served as quality examiner for the State of Florida, and published numerous papers on the subject of self-directed work teams. Frequent presenter at the ASTD and AQP National Conferences, the University of North Texas International Conference on Work Teams, and other national organizations. He has presented in Australia and Europe and conducts workshops on team building at local colleges and high schools. He is a member of the International Brotherhood of Magicians and the International Magicians Society. Ed has played on twenty world championship softball teams and has been selected to eight all-world teams. He was inducted into the Senior Player's Hall of Fame in 1999

Ed can be contacted at ed@myactorfactor.com.

* * * *

Dr. Lewis Losoncy

Lew Losoncy is a rare breed among psychologists, authors, speakers, trainers, and motivators. "Dr. Lew," as his many followers and fans know him, is internationally recognized for his ability to bring common sense answers to everyday situations and issues that often seem to bog people down and hold people back from taking control of their own lives and becoming successful. For more than two decades, Dr. Losoncy serves as an in-house psychologist for Matrix Essentials the largest manufacturer of professional beauty products in North America. Matrix is a division of L'Oreal, New York.

One of the world's leading authorities on the topic of encouragement, he has been dubbed "The Doctor of Encouragement" because the theme permeates his writing and speaking. A prolific writer, he has produced some 22 books and DVD's. His first major publication was *Salon Psychology: How to Succeed With People and Be a Positive Person*. He followed that with *Turning People On*, *The Motivating Team Leader*, *Best Team Skills*, and *Retain or Retrain: How to Keep the Good Ones from Leaving*. As the new millennium began, Dr. Losoncy wrote *If It Weren't for You, We Could Get Along: How to Stop Blaming and Start Living*; and created a set of DVD's dealing with *Attitude Modification*, followed by the books *Passionate Salon Professional* and *If It Weren't for Customers, Sales Would Be Easy!* Currently Dr. Lew is working on a new project entitled *Early Poppers: People Who 'Get It' and 'Make the Most of It!'*

Lew has conducted workshops in all 50 U.S. states, most of the Provinces of Canada, throughout Mexico, Australia, New Zealand, Thailand, England, France, Italy, Spain, and in Puerto Rico. One of his most recent engagements took him to Croatia. And one of the most interesting events occurred when he spoke to a group of Dell computer employees in Thailand – while he was simultaneously translated for the audience which spoke no English. He has been featured in such news media as *The Wall Street Journal*, *Psychology Today*, and *Working Woman*, *Prevention* and *Glamour* magazines. He has appeared on *CBS This Morning* and *CNN*.

Lew grew up in Reading, PA and spent most of his youth in that area. His undergraduate degree came from Kutztown State College. He earned his Master's degree and Doctorate from

Lehigh University in Bethlehem, PA. After teaching school and holding down a private psychology practice in Pennsylvania, he began an exciting life of travel that has seen him span the globe both for business and for pleasure. Lew maintains homes in Reading and Philadelphia, Pennsylvania and Indialantic, Florida, along with his wife Diane and daughter Gabrielle who attends Simon Rock College.

Contents

"To be or not to be: that is the question:

Whether 'tis nobler in the mind to suffer
The slings and arrows of outrageous fortune,
Or to take arms against a sea of troubles,
And by opposing end them?"

***Hamlet**, Act 3, Scene 1*
—William Shakespeare

"It's your decisions, not your conditions,

that determine your destiny."

— Anthony Robbins

Foreword

The books by Ed Rose have two things in common. They are about developing human capabilities, whether through individual effort or corporate intervention, and they evolve toward an increasing emphasis on the importance of choice. This book is about making choices or decisions about who controls your life. It is especially focused on the key decision to choose that control as the cornerstone of going through life. In that sense, it is rather Zen-like, focusing on the inner person and the power that can be tapped there. It is the power to determine the quality of one's experience by choosing the stance one takes in every situation, either to be at one's center or to be a victim.

Ed takes that a step further by articulating a variety of roles. Perhaps, the Director-ACTOR is most intriguing. In that case, the power tapped when you connect to your center frees you to relate to the rest of the world from a whole menu of possibilities, which then results in a whole banquet of positive outcomes. The key word is self-determination – freedom from having any exter- nal person or external stimuli pull your strings and determine your direction. It is not enough to live in a democracy; freedom or slavery occur as facets of every moment and every situation. We are conditioned by the advertising world to respond like dogs salivating to the sound of a bell. We are influenced by fast talkers and self-serving people and by status differences in all kinds of organizations. To the extent that we are other-determined, our lives remain shallow and meaningless. Richness of meaning and experience come with the shift to self-determination. A rich life depends on becoming self-determined.

Each of us is a unique center of experience. Each of us has a unique lens we look through when we engage with the world. Each of us has unique ways of contributing to those around us. That is diversity in its richest form, and it is a great asset to the organization and the community. A smart organization would nurture that uniqueness and find ways for its easy expression. When you put a whole group of self-determined people together, there is potential for a rich mix of talent and insight that cannot be matched. Everyone comes out a winner. You can't be part of that kind of community without becoming an ACTOR in the way Ed describes here.

Once you make the decision to live out of your own center, rather than give away your power to others, you have laid the cornerstone for building a life process that is rich with experience and also likely to be very successful in both tangible and intangible ways. Next, Ed describes five special facets of the self-determining ACTOR – adaptability, consideration, trustworthiness, optimism, resourcefulness – five ways to concentrate your attention and energy and time on crafting the relationships around you into a rich world. How is that possible? Ed provides examples, exercises, and quotes to meditate on to help you build the perspective, skill and habit of operating this way.

As you navigate life and the world, will you be the captain of your own ship? There is a lot of wisdom in this book about how to make yourself the captain. Some of that wisdom comes from Ed's experience, learning, and reflection, and more of it comes from a variety of people that Ed quotes. One definition of wisdom is the ability to learn from other's experiences. This book can take you up a good step on the wisdom scale, if you read it and think about it and practice it. I hope you enjoy being in charge of your own life and helping others do the same!

— **Dr. Michael Beyerlein**
Department Head and Professor
Organizational Leadership and Supervision
Purdue University

Preface

Choosing TO BE the Lead ACTOR in Your Life

Picture yourself in a continuous play for 80 years or so, on a constantly changing stage. You are the leading character in your play. Your rehearsals are those moments when you are learning your lines for the next act (planning your life). Reading this book is a good example of getting ready for the next scene in your play.

Think about some of the past roles and characters you have chosen to play in your life. For example, have you ever chosen to play a victim's role? Can you recall times when someone dominated you and treated you wrongly, and you wanted to yell and demand your rights, but timidly just kept quiet? Instead of being the ACTOR, you allowed yourself to be ACTED UPON by the other character in that scene. If so, do you sometimes, even today, still continue to play the victim in some relationships?

To Be the Actor, or To Be Acted On, That is the Question:

Do you remember when you played the role of an embarrassed person?

1. What did you think and tell yourself?

2. How did it make you feel?

3. What did you do?

In the play that is your life, it is important to remember that you also have another important role - that of Director. You are in control of how each scene plays out. Ask yourself, as director and leading character in your life's play, are there different things you could have achieved if you would have chosen instead to play a different role than that of an embarrassed person? To be the director and actor, rather than the one who was helpless and acted upon by outside circumstance?

Consider the same situation that "caused" your embarrassment, or more accurately, the same situation in which *you choose to play* an "embarrassed" role. What other role could you choose to play today if you had that scene to play over again?

1. What will you think and tell yourself today?

2. What will you feel about your experience today?

3. What will you do, and how will you act in your new role today?

To Act Out of Your Present Needs, or Out of Your Past Roles, That is the Question:

In becoming the Director-ACTOR in your life, you dramatically expand upon the limited range of roles from your past. Who says you have to be in the next moment the same person you where in your last moment? Plus becoming Director-ACTOR in your life, you gain the power of creation, of designing new thoughts, new emotions and new actions for your life. A new you created by you. You realize that you don't have to react to circumstances the same way you always have in the past. Instead of choosing helplessness, you can choose self-determination, and your new role will yield you new results. Instead of choosing to be a victim, you can choose to be the victor. Instead of being shy, you might walk back onto the stage of life as an outgoing person. You can choose spontaneity over a robotic response based on your past conditioning. You can say you act in life, rather than you react to life's circumstances.

Humans are quite different from the rest of the animal kingdom, because humans are not just passive products of their environment. The early study in psychology unfortunately made two errors that blocked our awareness of the human possibility. The first error that limited our beliefs in human potentials was to transfer the finding from Sigmund Freud's studies from very seriously disturbed individuals a century ago into your life today. Transferring studies results from one sample to a different type of sample is inaccurate. It would be like studying the NBA's average size ball players and concluding that the average size of a player is the general population. Again, early psychology was based upon a conclusion drawn from a limited sample and no implications in your life. Psychotic and neurotic individuals are not the lead

ACTORs in their life, but rather are controlled by anxiety, obsessions, delusions and hallucinations. You are controlled by your choices when you become an ACTOR.

The second error that squelched human possibilities was in the conclusions by the behavioral and experimental psychologists that if we studied animals like rats, monkeys, dogs, and pigeons, what we could learn form them would be transferred to your life. Yes, it's true that humans are animals; one part of human nature is animal nature, the need to eat and sleep and the potential conditional ability of our past experiences. There is another part of the human being that the ACTOR is cultivating and that is the human part. This includes the ability to think, feel, dream, plan, create, design and ACT in a self-determined way, not in an environmentally determined way.

You might think about it this way - animals simply respond to their environment based upon the conditioning from their past. An example of this in humans is the knee jerk reflex. If you tap the knee it will automatically respond. Human beings, unlike animals, are truly ACTORS in their life rather then being acted upon by the stimulus, therefore choosing their response.

Response. Can we prove this? Of course. If two children fail a test will both children be equally upset by their failure? Of course not. One might be totally devastated because of the failure or the stimulus while the other would say, I failed because I didn't put the right answers in the right place that time. The first child was acted upon that his response was a direct response to him looking at the test paper and seeing a failure. He didn't realize he had options to look at the failure, he allowed the stimulus to dictate his automatic response. He sees the F and feels as though he is a failure. The second child however chose to be the ACTOR rather than be acted upon. The second child was not stimulus response motivated but was what we will call stimulus YOU response motivated; that is, you see the stimulus as the Failure and then you think about it and choose your response. I failed because I didn't study and put the answers in the wrong place. If I want a better grade I had better study more and put those answers in the right place. The ACTOR sees a failure as a learning experience.

If 1000 people all experienced the same crises or setback in life, would all 1000 people be equally upset? Certainly not. Some would be devastated while others, after organizing their thoughts, would choose to act in ways that would overcome the setback and build their future. As a result, you can see that the ACTOR has a lot of advantages over the person who chooses to be acted upon because the ACTOR knows that no matter what happens to them in life they have the ability to choose their responses. The person who is acted upon does not have that option. The person who is acted upon has to wait to see what happens to them in their environment to see how good of a day they are going to have. In other words, when they wake up in the morning they don't know if it's going to be a good day or not because they don't know if the world is going to be nice to them.

You Are Writing the Script of Your Life:

What does all of this mean in a book called *The ACTOR Factor: Are You Ready to Take the Lead Role in Your Life*? Imagine your experiences in life as being part of a play and you are the ACTOR.

This play however is different from the plays in school or in acting class. Those lines had to be memorized and repeated the same way day after day. Chances are those lines in the scenes were written by someone else. The important play you are in today is quite different. This play is your life. And hopefully you are the lead character in the play of your life.

WHEN YOU CHOOSE TO BE rather than NOT TO BE THE ACTOR, you shape the direction of your destiny. When you act differently, the other characters in your play respond differently.

Don't they? In other words, you teach people how to treat you. You can choreograph the direction of your destiny or how your life plays itself out. For example, you can give yourself, the lead character in your play, a purpose, a dream, a goal. Have you noticed the only people that reach their dreams are the ones who have them? The reason is that you can't reach a dream unless you have one. Does the character you play in your life have a purpose? Also you can play the part with passion and feeling. You can act out of love, courage, determination and you can change your world today. By changing your world, you begin changing the world outside you because the moment you act differently, perhaps more assertively, you gain the respect of others. Not only do you play the role of ACTOR you also play another important role — that of Writer. In addition to acting and directing the role you play in life, you are also in charge of creating and scripting it. Your role will either be written by you, or the other characters in your play, including those elusive characters Luck, Chance and Fate. You will be a pawn in another character's hand and be a respondent rather than choosing to be acted upon, or choosing to be the ACTOR of your life. You will notice that the more you choose to be the ACTOR and the determiner of your life the less issues like Luck, Chance and Fate will enter into the picture. Today you can take 5 steps we will describe in order to become the Writer-

Director-Actor in your life. Your life will change immediately at this moment and you can determine yourself to change the role you play in your life's play. You can be the lead character and you will not have to make the mistake of limiting the vision of the future by something as narrow as the limited experiences of your past. Many thousands of people have consciously made the choice to vote "yes" for themselves to be the lead ACTOR in their life and walk out on the same old stage of life as a different character. You can too!

In Chapter 1 we give you an idea of what a world class ACTOR might look like. It's important to remember that all of us have something special inside of us. The ACTOR works toward developing that special something regardless of the forces in life working against them.

*   *   *   *

The
ACTOR
Factor

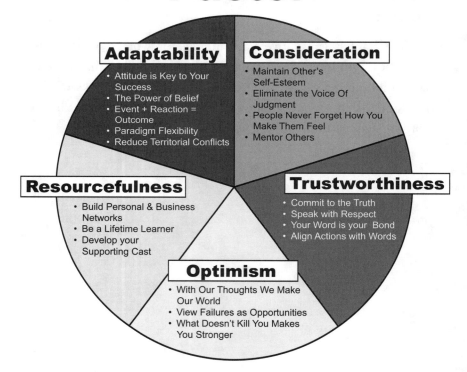

Adaptability
- Attitude is Key to Your Success
- The Power of Belief
- Event + Reaction = Outcome
- Paradigm Flexibility
- Reduce Territorial Conflicts

Consideration
- Maintain Other's Self-Esteem
- Eliminate the Voice Of Judgment
- People Never Forget How You Make Them Feel
- Mentor Others

Resourcefulness
- Build Personal & Business Networks
- Be a Lifetime Learner
- Develop your Supporting Cast

Trustworthiness
- Commit to the Truth
- Speak with Respect
- Your Word is your Bond
- Align Actions with Words

Optimism
- With Our Thoughts We Make Our World
- View Failures as Opportunities
- What Doesn't Kill You Makes You Stronger

Life Experience + The ACTOR Factor
= Success

CHAPTER 1

The Qualities of a World Class ACTOR

Lew Losoncy and I had many challenges in our lives and we both took control of our play. We met at the University of North Texas Work Team Conference in 1997. We quickly found that we shared the same positive outlook on life. In describing the world class ACTOR, we could have used each of our lives play. I drew the short straw.

In my life's play I have faced a lot of challenging scenes: abandoned at birth, failed in school, adoptive family was extremely poor, adopted father died when I was very young, I left home at 18, battled cancer, experienced a sudden layoff from my first job, and lost a very large amount of money by trusting a "friend" (at least I thought he was a friend). I almost forgot, I had to leave high school in the 11th grade because of pneumonia, but not because I had it, because I couldn't spell it! I joke about the fact I am poor speller. I consider that a weakness. In spite of it, I have authored 4 books and numerous articles and 30 team-building activities. As the ACTOR, I never let my weakness prevent me from accomplishing what I wanted to do. I believe I wrote the script of my personal play by being flexible enough to change when I recognized a change was required. Using the ACTOR qualities to create my own destiny, these qualities allowed me to build strong relationships with people in my life that helped me through the hard times and compensated for some of my weaknesses. One of my strengths was my ability to stay positive even in the time of extreme change. And above all, I always found a way to accomplish a task without making 101 excuses why it couldn't be done. In retrospect I realize that the foundation of my life was the network of support people (my supporting cast) that was made up of my coaches and friends.

During my early years, I associated with the wrong people. My mother and my new stepfather made an intervention and sent me to military school. The discipline of this school and the coaching I received there started to form a good foundation and allowed me to develop **ACTOR** qualities, i.e., **A**daptability, **C**onsideration, **T**rustworthy, **O**ptimism and **R**esourcefulness. Most of all, the coaching I received from Col. Dwight, the school president and football coach, may have had the strongest influence on my life. It wasn't until many years later that I realized that the coaching and support from Col. Dwight and other teachers had made such a positive impact on my life. My support group provided me guidance in my early years and feedback on how to improve. The influence of the support group and the people that I associated with built a strong values and beliefs system. I started to realize what my parents had been telling me for years. They would always say, "Son, you will become just like the people you associate with so choose your associates carefully." I realized from my own experience that their words were so true.

Choosing who you associate with, whether in work, life or athletics, might make the difference in success or failure. The same can be said for choosing a role model. It should be someone who is successful and has an optimistic outlook on life. I used my coach Col. Dwight as one of my role models. We both had grown up poor in south Jersey and both were fierce competitors. I can remember him telling me that I reminded him of himself when he was a young man. I believe that is why he became my mentor/coach in life as well as on the field.

Even ACTORs need a coach and role model. They must choose their supporting cast carefully. As Anthony Robbins once said, "Choose your friends and associates wisely because you become just like the people you associate with."

I have never forgotten Col. Dwight's philosophy on the world. He said, "Son, the world is like a cafeteria line, you can get anything you want. However, no one is going to bring it to you, and you have to pay the price." The ACTOR qualities deal with life in the same metaphoric sense in respect to individual success. You get what you put into it; you have to pay the price. You will always have to do it yourself, but you don't have to do it alone. In general terms, society may predict your destiny, but only you can determine it.

World class ACTOR s come from all walks of life. They are not special or gifted people. They are people who decided to take control. We will share a few examples of famous people that have chosen to be the ACTOR s in their life:

Anthony Robbins — Only has a high school diploma and who is most likely the richest motivational speaker in the United States today. He has consulted with presidents and makes millions of dollars. He works in a field without an advanced degree but is extremely successful. I have a special interest in Anthony Robbins. I have attended his Walking on Hot Coals seminar with one of my sons. I certainly recommend any other Robbins seminars. Anthony has certainly found and developed that something special inside of himself. He shares it with others. ACTORs will not regret spending time with Anthony. He is a great speaker and knows how to reach out and connect with people. Anthony has numerous workshops and books out and we recommend them to all ACTORs.

Oprah Winfrey — Life has thrown numerous challenges to Oprah and she wrote her own play. A lady with much grit in her life and her focus is to help others today.

Eleanor Roosevelt — Grew up being mistreated by family and friends because of her looks. People usually had negative things to say about her looks. Her legacy is she worked for those less fortunate. She is famous for the statement "No one can make you feel inferior without your consent."

Hillary Clinton — She chose to make her own decisions in life and not let the public do it for her.

Les Brown — Another story of a poor boy that his teachers said would never make it because he could not be educated. He went on to be a radio talk show host, politician and is also a highly regarded motivational speaker.

Alvin and Calvin Harrison

Alvin and Calvin Harrison — Twin brothers who won the gold medal in the 2001 Olympics. Alvin and Calvin grew up in a crime-ridden area of Orlando, Florida, but chose to be ACTORs in their lives with a little help from their supporting cast, their Grandmother. Read their story *Go to Your Destiny* (Hyperion, New York).

Tim Wakefield — Of the Boston Red Socks, a knuckle ball pitcher. He grew up with my sons. Tim was the director and ACTOR in his play. He wanted to play major league baseball, but he hurt his pitching arm in high school, so he decided to focus on hitting and went to junior college on a scholarship but was cut by the coach who said he couldn't make it. He had a different opinion and went to the Florida Institute of Technology and led the team in home runs. He was eventually drafted as a home run hitter in the minor leagues. He was about to be cut and decided to give pitching a try with his knuckle ball. Tim made it to the pros, where he faced additional challenges, but he is doing well with a great contract. Tim went on to win more games than any pitcher in Red Sox history and helped them win their first World Series in 80 years. He was the ACTOR-Director in his life.

Then there is the story of **Rudy Ruettiger** — you may have seen the movie *Rudy*. The young Rudy had a dream to play football at Notre Dame University. He was a very small boy, as football players go, and had very little athletic ability. In addition he wasn't a great student in the grades department. He had his dream and he wouldn't let go of it. He attended Notre Dame and holds the honor of being one of the few players ever to be carried off the field by the other players. He wrote and directed his own play.

What about **Rulon Garner** — a farm boy from the U.S. who won the Gold medal in the 2000 Sydney Olympics for wrestling. He beat Alexandu Karelin, who was 61-0 and three time world champion. The last time he faced Rulon he beat him 12-0. Rulon is the ACTOR in his life. He stayed focused, he dreamed, worked hard and went after his dream.

We could go on and on with examples. What most people, including myself, don't stop to realize is that once you believe something is possible it is in that moment that it becomes possible. Although I move through life with some of the ACTOR qualities, it wasn't until late in life that I fully took charge of it — at 48 years of age I started to write my own play. This is how I finally decided to become a magician after years of saying things like, I'm not smart enough, I'm not good with my hands, or it takes to much work, etc. I decided I was going to do it and actually wrote a book about the art called *Presenting and Training with Magic*, published by McGraw-Hill in 1998. Our dream may not be to win a gold medal or make a lot of money — we all have different aspirations.

The ACTOR qualities will provide you with metaphors for being an effective person and help you interact with other successfully while writing your life's play. The acronym ACTOR will remind you on a daily basis the basic ingredients for successful interaction with others.

It's time for you to decide if you are going to be an ACTOR or if you are going to be acted upon.

Just before publishing I came across this study that I feel emphasizes the need for being adaptable in order to reduce stress from territorial conflicts, subsequently benefiting your health.

Ask anyone what the most common symptom of a heart attack is, and most people will say "chest pain." Well, this is incorrect. The most common symptom of a heart attack is sudden death.

It can happen completely out of the blue, and many of you probably know of someone in your life who was trim and fit with none of the typical heart attack risk factors — no high cholesterol, no high blood pressure, a healthy eater, and a regular exerciser — yet died suddenly of a heart attack.

Your physical health is a direct manifestation of the various conflicts you've faced throughout your lifetime, along with your reaction to them.

This is not a theory or something to be discounted as "new agey."

This is the result of decades of focused, scientific work by some of the sharpest minds in the business: Dr. Geerd Hamer and Bruce Lipton. Their work has taken the widespread notion that your emotions influence your health (even the Centers for Disease Control and Prevention says that 85 percent of diseases have an emotional element) to a much higher, more specific level.

How a "Territory Conflict" Can Give You a Heart Attack

Let's say the recent mortgage crisis has caused you to lose your home, or you recently lost a close family member. Both of these territorial losses have signaled your body that you're under stress and to "get ready for a fight."

During this first phase, your coronary artery is actually made larger to get more of your blood flowing, and to help you win your upcoming "battle." Once your conflict is resolved, perhaps you find a way to keep your house, or you talk through your feelings of grief over your loved one's death, your body moves into the second, restoration phase, and will begin to restore your artery to normal size.

As Dr. Holt the famous cardiologist says, this can lead to a rise in cholesterol, which occurs to "spackle" the nooks in your coronary artery. And it is around this time, during your resolution of your emotional conflict, that a heart attack can occur.

The severity of your heart attack will be directly related to the length of time that your territorial conflict festered.

Stop Dwelling and Start Resolving Your Emotional Conflicts!

It is imperative that you tend to all of these emotional conflicts as soon as possible, since research shows that if you go longer than nine months with a moderate to severe territorial conflict, it is likely you won't survive the heart attack that follows.

A classic example is an executive who has felt his "territory" at work threatened by a younger member of the workforce for many months or even years. Then, upon their retirement — when the conflict has finally been resolved — they experience a massive heart attack.

Now, here's the kicker.

Sometimes a conflict is so extreme that you know you've been emotionally impacted immediately. But, oftentimes, you may have no idea.

In many cultures, we are taught to suppress our emotions, and to "grin and bear it." Well, little did you know, but those underlying resentments, arguments, regrets and guilty feelings can all manifest into disease over time. So, please, find a method of real stress relief and use it regularly — whether you think you need it or not. My particular favorite is the psychological acupressure technique the Emotional Freedom Technique (EFT), as it's simple to use and extremely effective.

Vote yes for yourself to be the Lead ACTOR in your life:

❏ **ACTOR**

❏ **ACTED UPON**

Everyone is told how important it is to vote. The presidential election of 2000 clearly proved that to be true. The election was so close. George Bush became president because of the vote of one Supreme Court Justice. In an election where 100 million people vote, each vote isn't likely to be the deciding vote. Wouldn't it be motivating if our one vote could be the deciding vote?

There is such an election. Each and every day you vote in an election that impacts your life even more significantly than whoever becomes president. This election is to vote YES for yourself each day to be the ACTOR, rather than to be acted upon. And in this election only one person votes — YOU DO. You are the deciding vote in the most important election of your life.

This book is designed to help you to change not just the actions in life, but to change you. When you change yourself, you change your life. If you begin now, rather than tomorrow, you will be a day ahead.

CHAPTER 2

Adaptability — Challenging the Process

ACTOR

Choosing to be the actor in your life...

❏ **Acted Upon:**
Rigidity
Return to the past
Inflexibility

❏ **Actor:**
Adaptability

"Things do not change; we change."
— **Henry David Thoreau**

"If you're going to create long-term change, you must believe that it's your responsibility, not anyone else's."
— **Anthony Robbins**

* * * *

Think of some people in your neighborhood or at work who resist change. What is their attitude? What does their body language look like? How do you feel when you are around them? If you ran a company, would you hire them?

11

Think of someone in your neighborhood who is open-minded and enthusiastic and loves to try new things. How do they look at things differently than the closed minded person? Our guess is you prefer being around this upbeat person more, don't you? Would you hire this person if you ran a company? Wouldn't you invite this person to your parties because they would be interesting, energetic and alive. The difference is, the second person voted "yes" for themselves and voted to become Adaptable in changing times rather than become antiquated. Now think of a time in your life when you were at the ballot box or at a point in which you had to select either being rigid, inflexible and resistant, or open, flexible, growing and learning. Can you recall a few times in your past? Do you remember when you made the stagnation choice? What results did you get? Can you recall a time in your life when you made the grow choice, you opened up your heart and your mind and you let change in. What results did the Adaptability choice give you?

The creative psychiatrist Otto Rank concluded that life is a series of choices. We are always at a choice point — one choice representing the stagnation into the safety, security and predictability of the past or what we believe to be safe and predicable. The other choice represents growth and accepting change. Rank believed that the quality of our life was a result of the choices that we made at these points.

A person should be comfortable with change and understand that change is happening all around them. Charles Darwin said, "It's not the strongest of the species, nor the most intelligent, that survive; it's the ones most responsive to change." If we think about what he was talking about, it becomes easy to draw the analogy to being a person who is not locked into their position in a conflict so tightly that they lose their objectivity. Even successful companies once on the Fortune 500 list who failed to recognize that change was required, met failure in the 1980's. A total of 230 companies disappeared from the Fortune 500 list in the decade of the 80's. Just like those companies, we, as individuals, must have the element of adaptability to be effective, and the foundation of adaptability is a positive mental attitude. As Epictetus said back in 60 AD, "It's not what happens to us that affects us, it's our attitude towards it, that does." And John C. Maxwell said, "Attitude is the speaker of our present; it is the prophet of our future."

Can that be? Can our lives actually be enhanced by altering our attitudes? Does success or failure have anything to do with mental attitude?

Television personality and author Art Linkletter would respond affirmatively. Linkletter said, "Things turn out the best for people who make the best out of the way things turn out." From Epictetus to Linkletter, the theme is the same — it's your attitude that is the key to your success. To be adaptable you must have a positive attitude. If you start with the articulation of a positive attitude it will affect your own well being. If you tell yourself you feel good, for example, before long you will start to believe it. Your conscious, deliberate, determining mind tells your obedient, compliant, subconscious mind to put a smile on your face and a brighter step in your feet. The Actor decides to turn the down day around. The one who is acted upon finds reasons to stay down, even digging themselves into an even deeper hole. The power of belief has the ability to create or destroy, and the good news is that empowering yourself is all up to you. As an adaptable team member it is most effective if you choose to have a positive attitude towards your team's goals and activities. Choose to maintain a positive mental state for paradigm flexibility in planning and problem solving. There are always perceptual alternatives. Bertrand Russel observed, "in the vast realm of our alive, creative minds there are no limits." We find too many times that we take action before taking time to plan. You could say that "failing to plan is planning to fail." ACTORs take up-front time to plan before implementing action. Open and honest communication with others needs to be developed. Your attitude can be considered the control panel of your life. It affects even the quality of your life. The one thing you have total control over in your life is your attitude. You choose it, and it will affect you in everything you do and will become a major factor in your ultimate personal success or failure. Your attitude is just a reflection of who you are on the inside. The amazing thing is, almost like a mirror, people around you respond to your stimuli. This reminds me of a story I heard some time back about these two young ladies working in a local community hospital. They decided to quit because the people were just too hard to get along with; they were always complaining and seemed ungrateful. In addition, the staff always seemed to talk behind each other's backs. The day before they were to leave they decided to try an experiment. They treated everyone with encouragement and praised them whenever they could. It was like a miracle the way the patients and staff changed. What these two women experienced was the golden rule: "treat others like you would like to be treated yourself." The situation change was caused because their attitudes changed.

Professor Erwin H. Schell, one of America's most respected authorities on leadership, said, "Obviously, there is something more than facilities and competence that makes for accomplishment. I have come to believe that this linkage factor, this catalyst if you will, can be defined in a single word — attitude. When our attitude is right, our abilities reach a maximum effectiveness and good results inevitably follow."

The importance of attitude on your future cannot be understated. To be an effective member of a team, and for your personal success in the long term, it is essential to have a "can do" attitude. Moving with the advantages of certainty produces an enthusiasm that others can sense. The message is simple; circumstances are uncontrollable, both in your job and outside environment. Things just happen. Hurricanes and tornadoes will arrive when they want to, not when you want them to. Your responsibility is to choose your responses to these circumstances. And your attitude is your toolbox to help you cope. Situations may color your views about teamwork or other issues, but you have been given the power to choose what color you want to make it. When we talk about attitude, most people say they have a good attitude. Only you know the answer to that. The test of an attitude is when things go bad for you ... how do you respond? Remember the equation E+R=O: Event + Reaction = OUTCOME. Very simple, but it is the foundation for being adaptable and it allows you to challenge the process. In the broad sense, how you look at the world determines how you adapt to it.

FOR EXAMPLE:

I recently overheard a friend of mine telling another about how helpless we are today in this rapidly changing world. "The older I get, the more the world around me has changed. They now make alcohol a lot stronger than they used to, the kids are louder and more energetic, and unlike the music I grew up with, it's just loud, meaningless noise. There must be some chemical in the water like a narcotic, because I am getting tired more easily. Food has definitely gotten fattier and it's harder to keep fit than it was five years ago. I can't figure it out."

My defenseless friend had nothing to do with his powerlessness in this difficult world. He sees the world through the veil of his attitudes, which he considers to have no control over.

To challenge the process one must be willing to look on the bright side of a situation. Challenge the old ways of doing things, and use what Joel Barker calls "Paradigm Flexibility." Look for ways to create new solutions to old problems. Be willing to take calculated risks.

Let's test your Paradigm Flexibility with the following:

**TASK: Move three and put two back
making the same design**

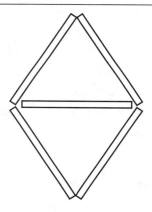

Now let's see what you learned from that exercise. Make the following Roman numeral into the number 6 using only one line:

IX

The answers to these problems are in the back of the book [P. 162}.

So how did you do? Do you think you have paradigm flexibility, or could you improve?

Was the task hard or easy? Did you make it harder than it had to be because of the way you interpreted the questions? How did you define "move three, and put two back"? There are no right or wrong answers here, just thought provokers for you.

Action question for you: What could you change today that would make you more effective?

_____

_____

What actions will you take to make your change?

_____

_____

_____

Lets look at what Adaptability is, and what it isn't.

Actor:

> Flexible
>
> Willing to adjust
>
> Open-minded
>
> Embraces change
>
> Paradigm flexibility
>
> Looks for new solutions
>
> Looks for opportunities

Process-oriented

Aware of their abilities

Regulates self in team meetings

Sees problems as opportunities

Acted Upon:

Rigid

Reluctant to change

Closed to other's ideas

Resists change

Paradigm paralysis

"If it ain't broke, don't fix it"

Sees opportunities as problems

Outcome oriented — "the end justifies the means"

Sees no need for self-awareness

Self-Awareness … just how important is it? Tao said, "If you know your enemy you will win 1,000 battles … if you know yourself you will never be defeated."

Adaptability is founded in your ability to be self-aware of what needs to be changed!

Adaptability

Attitude is EVERYTHING.

> *"The key to your universe is that you can choose."*
> **—Carl Frederick**

"A clear understanding of negative emotions dismisses them."
— Vernon Howard

> *"Your living is determined not so much by what life brings you as by the attitude you bring to life."*
> **—John Homer Miller**

"When things go wrong don't go with them. Think things through then follow through."
—Eddie Rickenbacker

> *"The greatest discovery of my generation is that human beings can alter their lives by altering their attitudes of mind."*
>
> *"We can't direct the wind, but we can adjust the sails."*
>
> *"Acceptance of what has happened is the first step to overcoming the consequences of any misfortune."*
> **—William James**

"You are searching for the magic key that will unlock the door to the source of power; and yet you have the key in your own hands, and you may make use of it the moment you learn to control your thoughts."
—Napoleon Hill

"Lord, grant that I may always desire more than I can accomplish."
—Michelangelo

"Things turn out best for the people who make the best of the way things turn out."
—John Wooden

"Have a purpose in life, and having it, throw your work such strength of mind and muscle as God has given you."
—Thomas Carlyle

"What looks like a loss may be the very event which is subsequently responsible for helping to produce the major achievements of your life."
—Skully Blotnick

"If you greatly desire something, have the guts to stake everything on obtaining it."
—Brendan Francis

Persistence

"Your persistence is your belief in yourself."
—Brian Tracy

> *"I think and think for months and years. Ninety-nine times the conclusion is false. The hundredth time I am right."*
> **—Albert Einstein**

"The harder you work the harder it is to surrender."
—Vincent Lombardi

> *"The only time you can't afford to fail is the last time you try.*
>
> *Nothing in the world can take the place of persistence.*
>
> *Talent will not ...*
>
> *Nothing is more common than unsuccessful men with talent.*
>
> *Genius will not ...*
>
> *Unrewarded genius is almost a proverb.*
>
> *Education will not ...*
>
> *The world is full of educated derelicts.*
>
> *Persistence and determination alone are omnipotent."*
> **—Calvin Coolidge**

"I start where the last man left off."
—Thomas Edison

"Do not despise the bottom rungs in the ascent to greatness."
—Publilius Syrus

*"Failure is only the opportunity to begin again
more intelligently."*
—Henry Ford

Purpose

Our greatest need and most difficult accomplishment is to find true meanings in our life.

*"To work at things you love, or for those you love, is to turn
work into play and duty into privilege."*
—Parlette

*"You have to do it yourself. No one else will do it for you. You
must work out your own salvation."*
—Charles E. Popplestone

*"Visualize this thing you want. See it, feel it, believe in it.
Make your mental blueprint, and begin to build."*
—Robert Collier

*"Nothing splendid has ever been achieved except by
those who dared believe that something inside of
them was superior to circumstance."*
—Bruce Barton

When skill and love work together, expect a masterpiece!
—John Ruskin

Courage

"Courage is the first of human qualities because it is the quality which guarantees all others."
—Winston Churchill

"Courage is resistance to fear, mastery of fear — not absence of fear."
—Mark Twain

"Don't be afraid to give up the good to go for the great."
—Kenny Rogers

"Only when a tree has fallen can you take the measure of it. It is the same with a man."
—Anne Morrow Lindbergh

"Courage is doing what you're afraid to do. There can be no courage unless you're scared."
—Eddie Rickenbacher

"Courage follows action."
—Mack Douglas

It takes courage to push yourself to places that you have never been before... to test your limits... to break through barriers.
—Anais nin

Creating Destiny

We become what we think about. Life is a self-fulfilling prophecy.

"Concentrate on where you want to go, not on what you fear."
—Anthony Robbins

*"Life can only be understood backwards,
but it must be lived frontwards."*
—Kierkegaard

*"The greatest thing in the world is not so much
where we stand as in which direction we are
moving."*
—Oliver Wendell Holmes

*"To love what you do and can feel that it matters — how could
anything be more fun?"*
—Katherine Jackson

*"Always think of what you have to do as easy and it will
become so."*
—Emile Coué

Mission

*"Whatever you are by nature, keep to it; never desert your line
of talent. Be what nature intended you for and you will
succeed."*
— Sydney Smyth

"We must not only give what we have; we must also give what we are."
—Desiré Joseph Cardinal Mercier

"We must believe that we are gifted for something, and that one thing, at whatever cost, must be attained."
—Marie Curie

"Peak performers create their own missions. They do it first by determining what they truly care about, then devoting themselves to the pursuit."
—Charles Garfield

"We're not all designed to be straight A students, celebrities, world-class athletes or the CEO of a major corporation, but we are designed to make the most of the skills and abilities we do possess. Perhaps the most splendid achievement of all is the continuing quest to surpass ourselves."
—Denis Waitley

CHAPTER 3

Consideration — Encouraging the Heart

ACTOR

Choosing to be the actor in your life...

❏ **Acted Upon:**
Lacks feelings and caring for others
Makes fun of / judges others
Thinks their ideas are more valuable than other's
Sees emotion as weakness

❏ **Actor:**
Consideration

"Men, as well as women, are much more often led by their hearts than their understandings."
—**Lord Chesterfield**

"Right words ... the resulting effect is physical as well as spiritual and electrically prompt."
—**Mark Twain**

Sometimes the difference between success and failure to individuals is the level of consideration used in personal interactions. Consideration is adaptability to people, like adapt-

27

ability is openness to circumstances. Both are important qualities present in the happiest, healthiest humans or what A.H. Maslow calls "self-actualization." Developing your consideration qualities may require some personal changes.

First, consciously force yourself to eliminate the Voice Of Judgment (VOJ) from your thought process. The VOJ is that little voice that pops up in your head when someone says something that appears to you as strange or different from your way of thinking. The VOJ can and does stop most creativity on a team. Let's take a minute to test your VOJ. I will ask you to make a decision on two situations based on what you believe. Make a decision so you can experience my metaphor on the VOJ.

Please decide:

1. If I asked you to make a decision on whether you would recommend that this person have another child or not, what would you recommend?

    The woman has 8 kids already, three who were deaf, two who were blind, one mentally retarded, and she has syphilis. Would you recommend she have another child?

2. We want to select a good leader. Study the following candidates … who would you choose to follow? Here are the facts about the three leading candidates:

    Candidate A: Associates with crooked politicians and consults with astrologers. He's had two mistresses; chain-smokes and drinks 8-10 martinis a day.

Candidate B: He was kicked out of office twice, sleeps until noon, used opium in college and drinks a quart of whiskey every evening.

Candidate C: He is a decorated war hero. He's a vegetarian, doesn't smoke, and only drinks an occasional beer.

Which of these candidates would be your choice?

* * * *

These questions were developed to see how effective we are in making judgments based on limited knowledge. One of the questions deals with values and beliefs just as your VOJ. These questions are being used as a metaphor for your VOJ. If you have participated and made your choices, evaluate your personal VOJ.

VOJ has limited knowledge and using it does have negative effects on working with people. The following are the names of the candidates described. What do you think of your selection? What does this tell us about judging people?

* * * *

Candidate A is Franklin D. Roosevelt

Candidate B is Winston Churchill

Candidate C is Adolph Hitler

* * * *

And, by the way, in answer to the pregnancy question — if you said she shouldn't have the child, the world would have lost Beethoven!

So our voice of judgment can be off as you most likely experienced in these two questions.

Consideration for others allows you to value the diversity of other's thoughts and opinions.

We all have to make judgments in our lives. The important thing when it comes to people is to make sure you have all the data before you make a decision. Eliminate your VOJ. You develop your consideration for others by softening your VOJ. Truly listening to another to really understand his or her viewpoint is tough and requires the development of 1) Inner security, 2) Openness, 3) Flexibility, 4) Creativity, and 5) Sensitivity. But the rewards and the fresh new view of life are worth it. Psychologists call this important quality "a tolerance for ambiguity."

Another example of consideration is helping others. You just never know when helping another can come back to help you. Consider this short story:

His name was Fleming, and he was a poor Scottish farmer. One day, while out trying to make a living for his family, he heard a cry for help coming from a nearby bog.

He dropped his tools and ran to the bog. There, mired to his waist in black muck, was a terrified boy, screaming and struggling to free himself. Farmer Fleming saved the desperate lad from what could have been a slow and terrifying death.

The next day, a fancy carriage pulled up to the Scotsman's sparse surroundings. An elegantly dressed nobleman stepped out and introduced himself as the father of the boy Farmer Fleming had saved.

"I want to repay you," said the nobleman. "You saved my son's life."

"No, I can't accept payment for what I did," the Scottish farmer replied, waving off the offer.

At that moment, the farmer's own son came to the door of the family hovel.

"Is that your son?" the nobleman asked.

"Yes," the farmer replied proudly.

"I'll make you a deal. Let me take him and give him a good education. If the lad is anything like his father, he'll grow to a man you can be proud of." Fleming agreed.

In time, Farmer Fleming's son graduated from St. Mary's Hospital Medical School in London, and went on to become known throughout the world as the noted Sir Alexander Fleming, the discoverer of Penicillin.

Years later, the nobleman's son was stricken with pneumonia. What saved him? Penicillin

The name of the nobleman? Lord Randolph Churchill.

His son's name? Sir Winston Churchill.

This story demonstrates that you never can tell what impact helping others can have. It might even impact an entire generation. This story deals with physically helping others in a big way. Again, we use this only as an example. There are numerous ways of helping others: maybe just a little encouragement at the right time; appreciation of someone's actions, or the like.

Consideration is valuing the needs and feelings of others. Aristotle said, "Encouragement is oxygen for the soul." This is another way to demonstrate your consideration for others.

Respecting them as people while recognizing emotions and dealing with them effectively.

To develop your consideration qualities, look to build relationships. Focus on recognizing others and showing appreciation. Remember this simple rule adapted from Confucius' famous statement:

"People will forget what you said

They may not believe what they saw

They will never forget how you made them feel."

The Golden Rule for consideration is to always maintain the self-esteem of others.

> *"Without knowing the force of words, it is impossible to know men."*
> **—Confucius**

*   *   *   *

Consider some insights in "The ACTOR Factor":

Seven Phrases to Help You Encourage the Heart:

1. "You made my day because …."

2. "One of the things I enjoy most about you is …."

3. "I am impressed with …."

4. "You can be proud of yourself for …."

5. "You are doing an excellent job with …."

6. "I was impressed with the way you handled the … situation."

7. "You have really made a difference in this project/team by …."

Appreciating people can have a strong effect on the IGA in your body. The IGA is the bio chemical signal sent from your brain to your body telling it everything is all right. The higher the IGA the better, and sincere appreciation will raise your IGA level. This includes you appreciating someone else as well as being appreciated. Yes, showing appreciation, caring for others or animals will benefit your health.

A personal favorite story of mine is what I call the yellow ribbon story. I believe it originates from Jack Canfield's book, *Chicken Soup for the Soul* (Health Communications, Inc.). The story starts with a teacher who asks her students to give a yellow ribbon to someone they appreciate. One of the students gave his yellow ribbon to a young executive who sponsored the Junior Achievement Program. The young executive was appreciative of the boy's gesture. He thought hard about whom he would give the ribbon to because that was the rule. The person who received the ribbon must pass it on to another person. The young executive decided to give it to his hard-nosed boss who had mentored him in several projects and, even though he was very cold to him, he really appreciated his help and guidance. The senior executive was speechless. He now had to give it to someone. On his way home he decided to give it to his only son. When his son came in from school he stopped him and explained he had a yellow ribbon to give to someone he appreciated in his life. "I want to give this to you because I appreciate the way you have worked hard in school and for being a joy in my life. I know I work a lot and don't spend the time I should with you but I love you." The son started crying uncontrollably. "What's wrong son?" After a few minutes the son said softly, "Dad, you don't know what this means to me! I was about to take my life because I felt unwanted, I never thought you felt like that." Well, appreciation can play a large role in your life. It certainly did for the senior executive. Is there someone in your life you appreciate and don't tell him or her? If there is, during the next 2 weeks take time out of your busy schedule and get a little card or yellow ribbon and tell them how much you appreciate them. Explain to them that they should do the same thing with people in their life.

Actor:

Values other's needs and feelings

Respects others

Maintains other's self-esteem at all costs

Considers all ideas from others

Listens with empathy

Recognizes emotions in others

Shares information freely

Help others in time of need

Eliminates one's internal Voice of Judgment (VOJ)

Acted Upon:

Does not recognize needs or feelings of others

Makes fun of / judges others

Thinks others should be stronger

Thinks their ideas are more valuable than another's

Sees emotion as weakness

Doesn't see the value of recognizing emotions in others

Holds onto information (power)

Team Building

"'*You could be right,*' *can be the bridge to reducing conflict.*"
—Ed Rose

"*Never lose a chance of saying a kind world.*"
—William Makepeace Thackeray

"*Innovation is simply group intelligence having fun.*"
—Michael Nolan

---

*Quotes for Consideration contributed by Dave Bruno

"Diversity is the art of independently working together."
—**Malcolm Forbes**

"Focus on the problem, not the personality."
—**Ed Rose**

"Never doubt that a small group of thoughtful committed people can change the world; indeed it is the only thing that ever has."
— **Margaret Mead**

"Great discoveries and achievements invariably involve the cooperation of many minds."
—**Alexander Graham Bell**

"As a rule of thumb, involve everyone in everything."
—**Tom Peters**

"Coming together is a beginning; keeping together is progress; working together is success."
—**Henry Ford**

"There are precious few Einstein's among us. Most brilliance arises from ordinary people working together in extraordinary ways."
—**Roger Von Oech**

"Maintain and enhance other's self esteem."
—Ed Rose

"The welfare of each of us is bound up in the welfare of all."
—Helen Keller

T ogether
E veryone
A chieves
M ore

Team Power

*"In helping others, we shall help ourselves, for whatever good
we give out completes the circle and comes back to us."*
—Flora Edwards

> *"I recommend to you … that of flattering people
> behind their backs. This is, of all flattery, the most
> pleasing, and consequently, the most effectual."*
> **—Lord Chesterfield**

*"What is required is sight and insight—then you might
add one more; excite."*
—Robert Frost

> *"Build for your team a feeling of oneness, of
> dependence upon one another and of strength to be
> derived by unity."*
> **—Vince Lombardi**

CHAPTER 4

Trustworthiness — Modeling the Way

ACTOR

Choosing to be the actor in your life...

❏ **Acted Upon:**
Uncaring
Unreliable
Actions don't align
with words

❏ **Actor:**
Trustworthiness

Have you noticed that "T" is right in the middle of the acronym ACTOR? Why, of course, because that's the way it's spelled. More importantly (metaphorically speaking), it's worked to hold the other qualities together.

Trust is the foundation of all human relationships. You can put a pile of bricks one on top of the other and they can be knocked down easily. But if you put mortar between them, they can withstand the outside force. The mortar in human relationships is trust. Actors must develop healthy and positive human relationships to be effective in all aspects of life. You can earn trust in many ways. When you create an environment that allows others to feel safe, even to fail, it contributes to establishing trust. It requires you to place an emphasis on having your words in alignment with your actions or "modeling the way." Modeling the way is "walking the talk." Your words match your actions. Be clear about your values and beliefs. Modeling the way requires you to be adaptable and considerate of the thoughts and feelings of others. Doing what you say is the first step in developing the groundwork for trust. There is a saying that people may not believe what you say, but they will believe what you do.

Take a moment to experience how important trust is to you. Think of a person with whom you would like to spend some special moments. What qualities does he or she have? Is trust one of them? Most likely your answer is "yes". And who do your trust anyway? You trust people who, in the past, did what they said they would do. They borrowed money and paid you back. Trust is essential for strong, solid, lasting human relationships. I think of trust as having three levels. The first level, Trustworthiness, is experienced when someone says to you, 'I believe in you- you did what you told me you would do.' At this level you build reliability, a certain level of openness and create a foundation of integrity, i.e., you said you would do it and you did. They believe that you can be counted on to live up to your words in the future. Level 2 — this level is about Consistency. It's where you constantly keep your actions in line with your words. If you will always operate at this level, people know you can be counted on. You are good for your word. The difference from Level 1 to Level 2 resides in the history of one person's actions with another, building what Stephen Covey might call your "Trust bank account." You build this bank account from your interactions with other people and how they view your actions. Level 3 is the most powerful level of trust, I believe, the ultimate trust. Some may even call it "faith." Simply put, it goes beyond the facts. Have you ever had someone in your life reach a Level 3 with you? A significant other? A child? A mentor/coach? Grandparent, etc.? Someone who, even if the facts indicated something different, you believed them? A person who would go to their grave with a secret you shared with them? This is the highest form of trust, and if you are able to go to this level, consider yourself blessed. Remember, only Actors who are trustworthy themselves will be able to reach Level 3.

There is a definite difference from just believing and trusting in someone. I use an example in my leadership workshops where I pour water into a cup and tell participants I just made the water disappear. Then I ask, 'does anyone believe me?' I usually get one or two who do because they know I'm a magician. It's not hard to say, "I believe." So then I ask, "will one of you help me demonstrate your trust that the water is gone and let me tilt it over your head?" Usually I get one person to say "yes", again demonstrating the difference between trusting and believing. I then tilt the cup over their heads. This visual metaphor demonstrates how the person was able to get to Level 3 trust with me. They went beyond facts to believe that I could make the water disappear. I did not get them wet. The water was gone. I could tell you the secret to this trick, but then I would have to kill you — it's the Magician's Code.

As an ACTOR you must demonstrate respect for others in your words and actions (consideration). Respect is the glue that allows relationships to work. It is important that we value all individuals' inputs, even if they seem bizarre to our standards. From personal experience, I have been amazed when what I thought was a bizarre suggestion turned out to be a great approach to the solution of a problem. Creativity can only occur when we have nurtured an environment where people can be free to express themselves. When we are respectful of others we should be using consideration qualities. This generates mutual respect, which is the foundation of trust and is essential to move up on the levels of trust. Respect for others allows you to model the way and build a trusting relationship. In respect to problem solving we need to consider all options and, in some cases, be willing to take one step backwards in order to go forwards. Recognize other's contributions. Lead by example — be accountable for your actions, maintain and enhance other's self-esteem. Discipline yourself to perform at your best. To be trusted one must have integrity.

> *"The best effect of a fine person is felt after we have left their presence."*
> — **Ralph Waldo Emerson**

"The soul is dyed the color of its thoughts, and think only of those things that are in line with your principles and can be the full light of day. The content of your character is your choice. What you think and what you do is who you will become. Your integrity is your destiny ... it's the light that guides our way." — Heraclitus (Greek poet/philosopher)

How you interact with others speaks to your trustworthiness.

There are 3 key questions for ACTOR's to answer, and if you can answer "YES" to these questions, you will be "walking the talk," while modeling the way for your supporting cast.

1. Are you committed to excellence?

2. Do you care about others?

3. Can you be trusted?

Actors establish a network (supporting cast) that can also answer "YES" to these 3 simple questions. Building the foundation of trust in a relationship starts with the basic beliefs. If you use the basic rules for Actor's interaction with others, this will be in alignment and enhance your rapport with them.

1. Always look for ways to maintain other people's self esteem in all interactions.

2. When discussing an issue, stay focused on the issue and not the person's personality, i.e., that was a stupid idea, John. Focus on the idea. John, that certainly is an interesting idea of selling rocks as pets. How do you see it working?

Trustworthiness is the center of ACTOR. It supports the other qualities. Without it you will never build the supporting cast you need to create your own script in life. We kept this chapter simple because trustworthiness is not that complex. If you are going to model the way for anyone in your family, community or organization, you have to be true to yourself. Remember the three key questions and be able to have your supporting cast answer "YES" to those questions. Use the basic ACTOR rules of interaction in your daily life. Review the contrast of trustworthy and move on to optimism and resourcefulness. A quality of being trusted gives you an advantage in optimism and resourcefulness.

Actor:

Reliable

Cares about others

Committed to excellence

Actions are in line with their words

Open and honest with others

Accepts feedback to grow

Acted Upon:

Can't be counted on

Thinks only of themselves and task outcome

"Let's get this over with ...."

Actions don't align with words

Provides a mask to others

Sees feedback as criticism

Leadership

"The high destiny of the individual is to serve rather than to rule."
— Albert Einstein

"If we take people as we find them, we may make them worse, but if we treat them as though they are what they should be, we help them to become what they are capable of becoming."
—Johann Wolfgang von Goethe

---

*Quotes for Trustworthiness contributed by Dave Bruno

"Take time to deliberate, but when the time for action has arrived, stop thinking and go in."
—Napoleon Bonaparte

"Let us be at least as generous in judging others as we are in judging ourselves."
—O.S. Marsden

"You cannot teach a man anything; you can only help him to find it for himself."
—Galileo

"Change is the law of life, and those who look only to the past or present are certain to miss the future."
—John F. Kennedy

"If you would convince others, seem open to conviction yourself."
—Lord Chesterfield

"Always bear in mind that your own resolution to succeed is more important than any other one thing."
—Abraham Lincoln

Mastering Change

"What lies behind us and what lies in front of us are but tiny matters as compared to what lies within us."
—Ralph Waldo Emerson

"You begin by always expecting good things to happen."
—Tom Hopkins

"A hundred times a day I remind myself that my inner and outer life are based on the labors of other men, living and dead, and that I must exert myself in order to give in the same measure as I have received."
—Albert Einstein

"What we must decide is perhaps how we are valuable, rather than how valuable we are."
—Edgar Z. Friedenber

"Destiny is not a matter of chance; it is a matter of choice. It is not something to be waited for, but rather something to be achieved."
—William Jennings Bryan

"It is always your next move."
—Napoleon Hill

"Deep within man dwell those slumbering powers; powers that would astonish him, that he never dreamed of possessing, forces that would revolutionize his life if aroused and put into action."
—Orison Swett Marden

Love

"Love is above all the gift of oneself."
—Jean Anovilh

"Whenever you share love with others, you'll notice the peace that comes to you and to them."
—Mother Teresa

"New links must be formed as old ones rust."
—Jane Howard

"The moment you have in your heart this extraordinary thing called love and feel the depth, the delight, the ecstacy of it, you will discover that for you the world is transformed."
—J. Krishnamurti

"Treasure each other in the recognition that we do not know how long we shall have each other."
—Joshua Loth Liebman

"Live for another if you wish to live for yourself."
—Seneca

"And in the end the love you take is equal to the love you make."
—John Lennon/Paul McCartney

Optimism — Inspiring Others

ACTOR
Choosing to be the actor in your life...
❏ **Acted Upon:** Sees all the bad in a situation Looses focus after failure Sees life's problems as "why me?" Discourages others
❏ **Actor:** **Optimism**

Optimism is also rooted in your attitude and is connected to Adaptability. These qualities are not linear, but are more dynamic in their interaction.

Optimistic people don't have their heads in the clouds, expecting nothing to go wrong. Actually, optimists are eagerly anticipating challenges. That's when optimists really shine. Optimists are realists with a plan, and these upbeat people don't allow others to set perceived limits they are always ready to challenge biases. "As long as we believe something is impossible, it will be," Baruch Spinoza said that more than three centuries ago, and that philosophy is equally true today. Optimism works closely with attitude, but deals more with the power to envision and plan for a positive future by not letting perceived limitations stop you from being all that you can. One of Yogi Berra's memorable wise statements was that "You can't steal second base with your foot on first." Stand up!! Challenge yourself! Challenge your biases! Take risks … being optimistic requires you to take things as they are and make them work for you. It all starts with what you say to yourself. Proceed with the unbending conviction that your challenges have solutions. That is how Jonas Salk the discoverer of the polio vaccine proceeded, and that's the conviction that John F. Kennedy showed when he stated that we would send a man to the moon and bring him safely back to earth.

> *"We are what we think, all that we are arises with our thoughts. With our thoughts we make our world."*
> **—Buddha**

Thoughts are real things. Thoughts are bricks. They can be used to build or to destroy. Watch your thoughts because these bricks build your words. Your major job in life is to build words that will construct a positive, motivated you. Why? Because words are transformed into actions. Your actions, if done repeatedly, become your habits. Your habits comprise the foundation of your character. Ultimately your character determines who you are, and some might even say, will determine your destiny. When someone asks, "How is it going?" how do you respond? Just, "I'm okay, I guess" or "Being alive makes anything possible. I'm on my way up."

Imagine everyone you meet as someone who's looking for someone to inspire them. Be a "pick people up" kind of person. Communicate that "you can do it." It's up to you to envision the positive future and set out to create that future. As author Steven Covey asserted, "The Best way to predict your future is to create it."

Also, view failures only as a learning experience. Life's little problems become just bumps in the road that you will find a way to get over. Believe in what you are doing or saying. Live with a sense of determination and walk that extra mile to meet your goals. What you will do is discover the best in you by giving your all. Your enthusiasm will be contagious and others will catch what you have. Repeat these words:

"As he thinketh in his heart, so is he."
—Proverbs 23:7

Actor:

Envisions a positive future

Stays focused on their task

Positive outlook on life

Sees failure in terms of a learning experience

Gets involved and helps others

Sees life's problems as just bumps in road

Plays the cards that are dealt

Encourages others

Acted Upon:

Sees all the bad in a situation

Loses focus after failure

Talks mostly about the bad things in life

Sees failure as personal weakness

Likes to criticize rather than help

Sees life's problems as — "why me?"

Complains about the cards dealt them in life

Discourages others

I have included statements that can I think are really important and will help you look at the bright side of your life's play.

If you find yourself stuck in traffic, don't despair. There are people in this world for whom driving in an unheard of privilege

Should you have a bad day at work, think of the man who has been out of work for years.

Should you have a despair over a relationship gone badly, think of the person who has never known what it is to love and be loved in return.

Should you grieve the passing of another weekend, think of the woman in dire straits, working twelve hours a a day, seven days a week to feed her children.

Should you notice a new gray hair in the mirror, think of the cancer patent in chemo who wishes she had hair to examine.

Should your car break down, leaving you miles away from assistance, think of the paraplegic who would love the opportunity to take the walk.

Should you find yourself at a loss and pondering what life is all about. Be thankful. There are those who didn't live long enough to get the opportunity.

*Should you find yourself the victim of other people's bitterness,
ignorance, smallness, or insecurity, remember things could be
worse. You could be one of them.*

Solving Problems

*"There is no such thing as a problem without a gift ... you
seek problems because you need their gifts."*
—Richard Bach

*"What happens is not as important as how you react to what
happens."*
—Thaddeus Golas

"There's a way to do it better ... find it."
—Thomas Edison

"See things as you would have them instead of as they are."
—Robert Collier

---

*Quotes for Optimism contributed by Dave Bruno

"All you need is a plan, a road map, and the courage to press on to your destination."
—Earl Nightingale

"Great results cannot be achieved at once; and we must be satisfied to advance in life as we walk, step by step."
—Samuel Smiles

"Never, never, never, never, never, never give up."
—Winston Churchill

Success

"In order to succeed, we must first believe we can."
—Michael Korda

"Success is one percent inspiration and 99 percent perspiration."
—Thomas Edison

"To succeed it is necessary to accept the world as it is and rise above it."
—Michael Korda

"In all things success depends on previous preparation and without such preparation there is sure to be failure."
—Confucius

"The difference between a successful person and others is not a lack of strength, not a lack of knowledge, but rather, a lack of will."
—Vince Lombardi

We rise to high positions or remain at the bottom because of conditions we can control if we desire to control them.

Success

"To laugh often and much;

*To win the respect of intelligent
people and affection of children;*

*To earn the appreciation of
honest critics and endure the
betrayal of false friends;*

*To appreciate beauty, to
find the best in others;*

*To leave the world a bit better,
whether by a healthy child,
a garden patch, or
a redeemed social condition;*

*To know even one life has breathed
easier because you have lived.*

This is to have succeeded!"
—Ralph Waldo Emerson

*"When your desires are strong enough you will appear to
possess superhuman powers to achieve."*
—Napoleon Hill

*"It sometimes seems that we have only to love a thing greatly
to get it."*
—Robert Collier

"Throw your heart over the fence and the rest will follow."
—Norman Vincent Peale

"You can't start a fire without a spark."
—Bruce Springsteen

"Anything you really want you can attain, if you really go after it."
—Wayne Dyer

"Dream lofty dreams, and as you dream, so you shall become."
—James Allen

"Do your work with your whole heart and you will succeed — there's so little competition."
—Elbert Hubbard

"Think enthusiastically about everything, but especially about your job. If you do you'll put a touch of glory in your life. If you love your job with enthusiasm you'll shake it to pieces.

You'll love it into greatness. You'll upgrade it, you'll fill it with prestige and power!"
—Norman Vincent Peale

"Enthusiasm is the mother of effort, and without it nothing great was ever accomplished."
—Ralph Waldo Emerson

"Cherish your visions; cherish you ideals; the music that stirs in your heart, the beauty that forms in your mind, the loveliness that drapes your purest thoughts, for out of them will grow all delightful conditions, all heavenly environment. Of these, if you but remain true to them, your world will at last be built."
—James Allen

Positive Self-Image

"Self worth comes from one thing, a belief that you are worthy."
—Wayne Dyer

"Learn to value yourself, which means; to fight for your happiness."
—Ayn Rand

"The best things in life are yours, if you can appreciate yourself."
—Dale Carnegie

"Assert yourself to make a few mistakes. If people can't accept your imperfections, that's their fault."
—Dr. David Burns

"No one can make you feel inferior without your consent."
—Eleanor Roosevelt

"And above all things, never think that you are not good enough yourself. A man should never think that. My belief is that in life people will take you very much at your own reckoning."
—Anthony Trollope

"I have an everyday religion that works for me. Love yourself first and everything else falls into line. You really have to love yourself to get anything done in this world."
—Lucille Ball

"You have to believe in happiness or happiness never comes."
—Douglas Malloch

"Remember that happiness is a way of travel, not a destination."
—Roy Goodman

"Happiness is a conscious choice, not an automatic response."
—Michael Bartel

"Though we may search the world over for the beautiful we find it within, or we find it not."
—Ralph Waldo Emerson

"Those who bring sunshine into the lives of others cannot keep it from themselves."
—J. M. Barrie

"We have to learn to be our own best friends because we fall too easily into the trap of being our own worst enemies."
—Roderick Thorpe

"Be happy in the moment, that's enough. Each moment is all we need, not more."
—Mother Teresa

* * * *

CHAPTER 6

Resourcefulness — Enabling Others to Act

ACTOR
Choosing to be the actor in your life...
❏ **Acted Upon:** Allows emotions to control their reactions Allows situations to control them Thinks only in terms of one-way solutions to problems Builds barriers with others
❏ **Actor:** **Resourcefulness**

"We will either find a way or make one."

— HANNIBAL

We all know of Walt Disney, but did you know that Walt was fired from a newspaper for lacking ideas? He also went bankrupt several times before he built Disneyland. Walt certainly wrote his own life's play and he had to rely on his resourcefulness to accomplish it.

63

Resourcefulness is the last letter in the acronym ACTOR and symbolically represents the quality that one must have to accomplish their goals. The ACTOR must use all the qualities discussed in the previous chapters. However, it's resourcefulness that will make the difference in getting ahead and reaching your personal aspirations. Remember what Col. Dwight, my mentor and coach, said in our introduction? My mentor inspired me with the words and beliefs, "You can get anything you want as long as you are willing to get up and get it and pay the price."

Author David Joseph Swartz states the basic rule for achieving success depends on the support of other people. Henry Ford concluded, "I am not the brightest person in the world, but I will never miss an opportunity to use the brains and the resources of the people around me." So, as the ACTOR, being resourceful means more than just having a bias to action and a can-do attitude. An ACTOR works with people and is able to get the job done by being innovative and using breakthrough thinking while valuing the diverse ideas of others. An ACTOR who is resourceful will:

1. Enable others to act

2. Take initiative to ask for what they want (recommend reading the book, *The Aladdin Factor*, authored by Jack Canfield and Mark Victor Hansen. This book goes into details on the value of asking for what you want).

3. Put the network in your life together whether in personal or business life. This is very similar to what author Napoleon Hill stated in his book, *Think and Grow Rich*. A person must create a mind mastery

group to reach their goals. Hill's data indicated that we should form a mind mastery group of successful people that can help us succeed. We see that as simply a network of skilled people that work together to help each other.

In today's world of high technology and speed we are inundated with data. This is indeed the "Information Age," so much so that successful people and organizations must rely on the collective intelligence of individuals or your network. It is time to break down perceived barriers within organizations and relationships. Enabling others to act simply means that you use all the ACTOR qualities that promote collaboration among as many individuals as you can. In terms of Actors who are leading others, this would enable them to act by delegating, educating, providing information and being informative. To build your network of support people, or your support cast, if you will, one must always treat others with dignity and respect and build bridges rather than create barriers wherever possible (in the metaphoric sense).

As a leader you must possess the ability to build alliances. Let me try to explain with a contrast of two great generals: General George Patton and General Dwight David Eisenhower. Both of these men were great leaders and Actors, however Patton, who with his Third Army crushed the Nazis, was never able to move on to the next level of command because he was unyielding and ferocious in his interactions. He could never lead a complex alliance required to win the war. General Eisenhower had the ACTOR qualities and the special resourcefulness to build bridges with others and create an alliance that encouraged and supported a collective effort allowing many egos to work together. Actors must be able to build their supporting cast like General

Eisenhower. We will refer to that supporting cast as your network. Who is your supporting cast? Who could help you by becoming part of your supporting cast?

Resourcefulness also requires you to become a lifetime learner and always be open to new ideas. It has been said that smart people learn from their mistakes. Smart people learn from other's mistakes. Remember, you can't live long enough to make them all yourself. Just as with mistakes, all ideas don't have to come all from you. Unless you try to do something beyond what you have already mastered, you will never grow and truly be the learner. Lou Holtz said, "We have two ears and one mouth, so we should listen twice as much as we speak." Good advice! It's important to know your strengths and weaknesses as an ACTOR. Then you can accomplish anything with support from your supporting cast (network) with strengths in areas you are weak in.

Resourcefulness is more than just doing something ... consideration and optimism are essential elements to resourcefulness and they work closely together. Resourcefulness qualities have a bias to action working with people. If you are not using the other qualities you will never build a supporting cast that are empowered and act on their own.

The ACTOR will have to use the simple technique of asking for what you want. This is a basic tenet of being an ACTOR, to take control of your life. If you put off asking for what you want or sharing your feelings, you might end up like the gentleman in this story:

A young man named Tommy really liked a young lady named Sally. Tommy felt that it was love at first sight. However, he was a little on the shy side in sharing what he wanted. So he decided to send Sally something every day. He would either send her a box of candy, flowers or just a card, however he was so shy that he didn't even let her know that he was sending the gifts. He had them delivered by Al, the local delivery guy. This went on for a year. He finally got enough nerve to call her and ask if she would go out with him. She said, "I wish you would have asked me sooner, but I just married Al, the delivery man who brought me the gifts every day for a year." Don't let this happen to you as an ACTOR … ask for what you want and take action to get it.

The ACTOR, as a leader, works hard to develop others. By developing others they improve their resourcefulness by building a strong network. They will build relationships and leverage diversity to meet their goals. Building a network/supporting cast is essential for meeting your life's goals. Your network is your supporting cast. It supports you in good and bad times. It's important to build a network in all aspects of your life. This network could even be your personal coach. The people in your supporting cast or network are ones that can help you become successful while you help them do the same. The network is about helping all of its members. It's almost like Ying and Yang — there is a balance between enabling others to act and accomplishing a task that has to be done. Ultimately, the task may be your personal success, but an ACTOR always talks in the "we", not "I."

We all have to do it ourselves, but we don't have to do it alone. The example I like to use here is when I have a car problem I always ask one of my friends to help me solve it. Have you ever done that before? Share a few facts about a subject and ask if they can help you. Sure you have … we all do. Then when they have a problem in your area of expertise, they call you. The other kind of network is when the entire group has a specific focus and they help each other to develop by specific feedback and collaboration.

However, when it comes to work issues, we all change our behaviors. Why? I suggest it's the competitive environment set up in most work units in the past. Resourcefulness means being less focused on who gets the answer and more about how fast we can solve the problem to save the company money. Resourcefulness involves others at all levels. A person who is resourceful will enable others to act for themselves, allowing others to grow in addition to helping the ACTOR.

To be resourceful one must involve others in problem solving while fostering collaboration. Actors don't worry about who gets the right answer; they focus on getting to the solution by utilizing all the brains in the room. Resourceful people use the collective intelligence of all the people participating in problem solving to obtain the optimum results referred to as Synergy. Resourcefulness, as I said before, requires all the qualities of the ACTOR to work together in concert. It requires the ability to enable others to act. One should be in full control of their actions. It is not getting things done at the expense of others. It is more about getting things done with people. The best way to do that is to build a network (relationship) of capable people. Your success depends on the amount of time you spend developing your supporting cast (network). A key thing to remember when you are building your network: you can make more friends in a month by being interested in them rather than in ten years trying to get them interested in you (taken from *Roads to Radiant Living* by Charles L. Allen). However, please keep in mind it's not about pleasing people. Remember this story:

An old man, a boy and a donkey were going to town. The boy rode on the donkey and the old man walked. As they went along, they passed some people who remarked it was a shame the old man was walking and the boy was riding. The man and boy thought maybe the critics were right, so they changed positions. Later, they passed some people that remarked, "What a shame, he makes that little boy walk." They decided they would both walk! Soon they passed some more people who thought they were stupid to walk when they had a decent donkey to ride. So they both rode the donkey! Now they passed some people that shamed them by saying how awful to put such a load on a poor donkey. The boy and man said they were probably right so they decided to carry the donkey. As they crossed a bridge, they lost their grip on the animal and he fell into the river and drowned.

The moral of the story?

If you try to please everyone, you will eventually lose your ass!

Resourcefulness and enabling others to act doesn't mean you have to please people all the time. It's about using all the qualities of an ACTOR and going after what you want. Actors always respect people and never damage the self-esteem of others. When they deal with problems they focus on the issues, not the personalities.

Key things to remember when you start developing your resourcefulness qualities and network/supporting cast:

1. Success is measured in the achievement of specific goals, not in the number of hours or days spent getting there.

2. Successful people do what unsuccessful people won't.

3. Surround yourself with dream makers, not dream killers.

4. We rise to greatness by lifting others.

5. The only limits to life's opportunities are the ones you set.

6. Seek advice from successful people.

7. The true riches of life come naturally as we enrich the lives of others.

8. It's better to create a future we love than to endure one we don't.

9. Look at life through the windshield, not the rearview mirror.

10. Tell ten people over the next few months how much you appreciate them.

11. We only fail when we stop trying.

12. "It is the nature of man to rise to greatness if greatness is expected of him." — John Steinbeck

13. Great achievers are ordinary people with extraordinary ambition.

14. There is always another way around or over the mountain.

15. There is a passion in togetherness.

16. Never doubt that a group of sharing, caring and serving people can achieve the impossible.

Let's review Resourcefulness in the context of To Be the Actor or To Be Acted Upon:

Actor:

Chooses how they react to their emotions

Takes control of the situation

Looks at problems from different perspectives

Breaks down perceived barriers

Never stops being a question mark (inquisitive)

Builds bonds and leverages diversity

Develops others

Involves others in problem solving

Acted Upon:

Allows emotions to control their reactions

Allows situations to control them

Thinks only in terms of one-way solutions to problems

Builds barriers with others

Leaves school as a period

Doesn't build alliances

Setting Goals

"Unless you try something beyond what you have already accomplished you will never grow."
— Ronald Olson

"Follow your bliss. First say to yourself what you would be, and then do what you have to do."
— Epicetus

"Deciding to commit yourself to long-term results rather than short term fixes is as important as any decision you'll make in your lifetime."
— Anthony Robbins

"This one step ... choosing a goal and sticking to it ... changes everything."
—Scott Reed

"Visualize this thing you want. See it, feel it, believe in it. Make your mental blueprint and begin."
—Robert Collier

*Resourcefulness Quotes contributed by Dave Bruno

Turn Your Goals into Reality

"There is one quality that one must possess to win, and that is definiteness of purpose, the knowledge of what one wants, and a burning desire to possess it."
—Napoleon Hill

Mission

"Whatever you are by nature, keep to it; never desert your line of talent. Be what nature intended you for and you will succeed."
—Sydney Smyth

"The greatest thing in the world is not so much where we stand, as in which direction we are moving."
—Oliver Wendell Holmes

"We must not only give what we have; we must also give what we are."
—Desire' Joseph Cardinal Mercier

"We must believe that we are gifted for something, and that one thing, at whatever cost, must be attained."
—Marie Curie

"Peak performers create their own missions. They do it first by determining what they truly care about, then devoting themselves to the pursuit."
—Charles Garfield

Taking Risks

"There are periods when to dare is the highest wisdom."
—William Ellery Channing

"Faith and doubt both are needed, not as antagonists, but working side-by-side to take us around the unknown curve."
—Lilian Smith

"Start by doing what is necessary, then what is possible, and suddenly you are doing the impossible."
—St. Francis of Assisi

"Chance favors the prepared mind."
—Louis Pasteur

"The important thing is this: to be ready at any moment to sacrifice what you are for what you could become."
—Charles Dubois

"When love and skill work together, expect a masterpiece."
—John Ruskin

Risks & Reward

"I have learned from years of experience with men, that when a man desires a single thing so deeply that he is willing to stake his entire future on a single turn of the wheel in order to get it, he is sure to win."
— Thomas Edison

"The secret of success is learning how to use pain and pleasure instead of having pain and pleasure use you. If you do that you're in control of your life. If you don't, life controls you."
— Anthony Robbins

We believe by being an ACTOR you will create your destiny. That destiny will be whatever you choose it to be. Consider the words of Epictetus, a Greek philosopher:

"Tentative efforts lead to tentative outcomes, therefore, give yourself fully to your endeavors. Decide to construct your character through excellent action and determine to pay the price of a worthy goal. The trials you encounter will introduce you to your strengths. Remain steadfast and one day you will build something that endures, something worthy of your potential."

Remember the story of Ray Kroc, a relatively unsuccessful marketer of restaurant equipment, who didn't sell his first hamburger until age 52. At a time when many people prepare for retirement, Ray Kroc built McDonald's from a handful of hamburger stands into the world's largest food chain. So the ACTOR can start at any time, it's never too late!

"The belief that becomes truth for me is that which allows me the best use of my strengths, the best means of putting my virtues into action."
— Andre Gide

What about Dick Clark? Many people don't know how America's oldest teen got started. When Dick's older brother was killed during WWII, he first withdrew into a shell. He started listening to the radio to ease the loss of his brother. He started to dream about having his own radio show, and that led him to American Bandstand, and the rest is history.

I have just given you examples of some well-known people and you may be getting the idea that you really can do what you dream. Yes, that is what I'm saying and I say it from my own experience. I am certainly the last person who ever thought I would write a book. I first envisioned it, took action and it became a reality. If I die tomorrow, I have accomplished more in various areas than I every thought I would growing up. The power of Col. Dwight's words keep coming back to me about life being like a cafeteria line … you can get anything you want but you have to pay the price and go out and get it. He did forget one important thing … you first have to dream or decide what you want and then go out and get it.

So, what is it that you want to accomplish or change in your life? The bad news is that time flies, but the good news is you are the pilot … if you have time to take action.

So you say you tried before and it didn't work. I think Michael Jordan put it best when he said, "I have missed more than 9,000 shots in my career. I've lost almost 300 games. Twenty-six times I've been trusted to take the last shot and missed. I've failed over and over and over again in my life." He said that's why he succeeds (this was cited in a Nike advertisement). So what about you? Are you ready to follow your dreams whatever they may be?

> *"A person is not old until regrets take the place of dreams."*
> **—John Barrymore**

Action Plan:

1. What can you do to become an ACTOR in your life?

   _____

   _____

2. Is there something you always wanted to do but had the perception you couldn't?

   _____

   _____

3. Is there a place you always wanted to go?

   _____

   _____

Goal:

Action Required:

Goal:

Action Required:

> *"We are what and where we are because we first imagined it."*
> **—Donald Curtis**

The ACTOR Knows That ...

Adaptability:

A good leader will adapt to, influence and encourage the change throughout the organization. The world is changing and so must a company ... survival depends on employee adaptability.

Consideration:

If consideration were an investment ... it would provide tremendous returns.

Listening is the foundation of working with others ... respecting their ideas is the glue that holds the working relationship together.

Trust:

Trust is the foundation of all human relationships ... without it organizations will struggle. Leaders must be able to answer "yes" to 3 key questions:

1. Can I be trusted?

2. Do I care about others?

3. Am I committed to excellence?

Optimism:

Optimists view failure as only a learning experience.

The optimist always look for the "PONY."

Optimism is the fuel that drives organizations beyond adversity.

Resourcefulness:

You don't need all the answers ... just know how to find them.

There are more ideas around you than within you!

Build a network to succeed ... you have to do it yourself, but you don't have to do it alone.

*   *   *   *

Transition

Now that you have finished the first six chapters, you are ready to put *The ACTOR Factor* to work in your life. My motivation in writing this book was to help other people understand what I have learned in my sixty-two years of living and from observations of other successful people. I also want to clarify the term "successful people." In my mind that doesn't mean the person with the most money or toys or power. Success is very personal and must be defined by each individual. In all the things I have accomplished, I am proud of the fact that when I pass on to meet my Maker I will leave a legacy for my children, grandchildren and great grand children. My start in life was a challenge. Looking back, I wish my parents where alive to see what I have accomplished. I am most proud of my family and the positive impact I have had on others.

Let me share this short story with you: it happened just the other night after a high school basketball game where I recognized one of the referees as a player I had coached thirty-seven years earlier in midget football. He told me that his brother, who also played on the team with him, was living in Maryland, and he gave me his number. When I called him, he shared with me the various issues and challenges he had faced since I last interacted with him. He told me what an impact I personally had on his life. I realized then that I had in some small way been able to positively affect another individual, as many mentors had in my life. This is where I see the real success of *The ACTOR Factor* in your life. Make a difference in someone else's life by passing on that little special something to that person. Teachers do this every day of their working life. I certainly can't tell you what success is — I can only give you my point of view. I can assure you that these simple qualities detailed in this book, if used in your daily life, will help you be successful in working with people. And if you can work with people, you will be a success in what ever you choose.

Going into chapter seven you will see how these qualities can be used very effectively with teams — work teams. Work teams, sports teams, any type of teams. Chapter eight is "Motivational Nutrients for the ACTOR's Soul." I once heard a speaker talk about the value of motivation. When asked, "What good is a motivation session? It wears off and people forget." He responded, "It's just like brushing your teeth. You wouldn't think of just doing it once. It's good for you, so you keep doing it."

In that sprit I have included chapter eight so you can rejuvenate yourself as you feel the need.

CHAPTER 7

Building a Team of ACTORs Who Value the ACTOR Factor

In today's workplace, a fast, flexible workforce and complex problem-solving skills are required so that everyone can work as a team. As an ACTOR you become the ideal team member.

Working on a team is basically personal interaction rather than one-on-one. Let me ask you, "just what is a team?" Take a minute and think of your definition of a team. Have it in your mind? Here are our thoughts:

One definition we heard is "a number of farm animals harnessed together pulling a plow." While that may be true, team members in a workplace would certainly take exception to being compared to laboring animals. I would define a team as "a group of people learning, working and growing independently together to reach an identified goal." Would you agree?

Take a minute and list as many types of teams you can think of.

Did you identify football, baseball, soccer, basketball, bowling, tennis or ice hockey? Normally we find that people note these on their list, but did you include family, work units, firefighters, and ambulance squad, Army, Navy Seals or the Boston Symphony? These are also teams and require specific behaviors to be successful.

We all view success as "winning." When we talk about high performance teams in terms of the "win/lose" metaphor, it would mean that they have won a lot more than they have lost. Winning teams require winning members. This requires special people who take responsibility for their own actions and also result of the team's overall performance (ACTORs).

These "winning" (or high performance) teams require team members who work together to produce what no one person can. The technical term used is to produce synergy. That is where the sum of the whole is greater than the sum of its individual parts. Some would say it's where "2 plus 2 equals 5", or simply, we can do more by working together. Today's world requires "collective intellect," where we take the collective knowledge of a group to produce amazing outcomes. Today's Information Age is overwhelming to most people, and teaming allows us a new way to manage all this information in problem solving activities.

When properly used it has been proven that teamwork can be beneficial to any organization, as well as the individuals that make up that organization. It all relates back to "associating with the

right people." Whether you are building workplace teams or simply forming a "team" (network) of friends, you have built your
support team structure (your supporting cast). A team approach
(support group) will compensate for individual weaknesses and
can produce more than the members could produce individually.
Teamwork works for the individual members as well as for the
organization. The key is to use the right teams in the right places
for the right reasons.

Take a minute to think who makes up your Life's Team (your
life's play of characters). These are the people in your life that provide you with a network or support group (your supporting cast,
if you will). We all have supporting cast, even Bill Gates with his
billions. Some of your supporting cast has big parts and others
may only be prop hands, but still are vital to your success.

List your virtual team (support cast/network):

Your network is a virtual team, not usually a work team, although
it could be. Let's discuss teamwork in general terms.

Teamwork is both complex and simple. Any time you bring a
group of people together who think differently and have different
agendas and backgrounds, you are in for challenges. The outcome
of that experience is totally up to you. We will refer to this as the
dynamics of the team. All of these ingredients give the team a high
source of possibilities. The key is to control the group dynamics
to obtain the best results from the collective group. From person-

al experience with teams, I have found that creativity tends to decrease as the team size increases. There are many factors which make team members feel uncomfortable. If each team member becomes an ACTOR, choosing to write their own play, using the ACTOR qualities will promote successful team dynamics. Choosing to be an ACTOR gives you the power to be an effective person whether working on a team at work or play. You know that to be successful you must be able to interact successfully with people. The ACTOR qualities establish a strong base for successful interaction among people from any culture. This includes interaction with members of your supporting cast/network team.

Recognize that you are a one-of-a-kind person in this world. You can choose to be an effective individual and, in turn, become a person who can successfully work with others in a team environment. We have been socialized to be competitive in the workplace. I have heard the saying, "I could hire half the workforce in the U.S. to kill the other half." This statement indicates the competitive nature of the workforce. Successful teams require a work environment where members support each other and work together. Even in early stages of the development of man, people realized their chances for survival increased if they banded together to hunt, fish and gather food. They found it to be even more important than being the biggest and strongest individual.

In today's world, coming together as a team is very similar to the way things where done in prehistoric times. The difference is the dynamics involved in the teamwork.

A story comes to mind about Billy Graham that I would like to share with you. Billy was looking for a local post office in a small town. He came upon a young boy and asked, "Could you tell me the direction to the local post office?" The young fellow gave him the directions and Billy asked if he wanted to hear him speak tonight. The young man asked Billy, "What are you speaking on?" Billy replied, "I am going to tell all the people who come how to get to heaven." The young boy replied, "No, thanks. You don't even know how to get to the post office!"

The boy was dealing with a limited amount of knowledge, and based on his data, he made his decision. There are five negative behavioral patternings that will prove a roadblock in your team efforts.

1. Being a rebel looking for a cause. They might act like they are looking for change and growth, but they are actually against change. They are inflexible to new ideas and very blunt with others without consideration for their feelings. The ACTOR would write their script with Adaptability qualities.

2. Seeing the World in Black and White. This can be defined as seeing everything as strictly on its merits. There are no emotions, politics, sentimentality or favoritism that should enter into any decision. These people don't listen to others, and when they do it's in a judgmental way. Remember the VOJ (voice of judgment). These people should focus on Consideration.

3. Focuses on me, me, me. This is where people say one thing and do another. Their actions are not in line with their words. They view feedback as criticism. They can hardly be counted on to complete an assignment as promised unless they can get personal glory from it. They speak in terms of "I did this, I

did that." Focusing on the Trustworthy qualities would be an excellent place for this person to start.

4. It will never work attitude — these people see only the bad in a situation. The company is out to get the employees. They love to criticize, and when they fail, they focus on that failure rather than trying to learn from it.

5. Lone ranger mentality — this person thinks they can do it alone no matter how big the project. If they delegate they still micro-manage. They want to take credit for the work. They more or less destroy bridges rather than build them. They build barriers and try to create kingdoms of control. They don't build alliances within the organization or within their own life. This person should be focusing on resourcefulness qualities.

These five negative behaviors you most likely have recognized in a team you associated with in the past. I certainly have seen them in both the work teams I have known and the sports teams I've played on or coached. As an ACTOR you will be able to influence these people by your personal qualities. These ACTOR qualities can be contagious, and a winning team requires these qualities.

Let's take a minute to review the comparison between a Winning team and a High Performance team:

A model of a good team player:

Winning sports team	*High Performance work team*
Good athletic skills	Good job skills
Understands role	Understands role
Values other's contributions	Values others
Positive in adversity	Positive attitude
Prepare/Train	Study/Learn

As you can see, the attributes of a winning team are very similar to those of a high performance work team. The glue that keeps all this together is the attitude of the player/worker. Success is where good preparation meets opportunity with a positive attitude.

Choosing to be an ACTOR will give you control of your life whether you want to be successful as a team member or leader.

In Chapter 8, Motivational Nutrients for the ACTORs soul, we will share stories, parables, quotes and short exercises (nutrients for your soul). We recommend reading a quote or story a day, either in the morning or evening, to help you realize that what you have in your life has a lot to do with how you decide to vote today. Will you wake up in the morning and vote to be an ACTOR and say, "This is going to be the first day of the rest of my life and I plan to make the most of it." When someone asks you how do you feel today, tell them if you were any better the government would be charging you a luxury tax.

Enjoy!

If you have any stories you would like to share with us for our workshops please send to:

Ed Rose
edrose@cfl.rr.com

or

Lew Losoncy
llosoncy@aol.com

Now for your Action Plan ...

We believe by being an ACTOR you will create your destiny. That destiny will be whatever you choose it to be. Remember the words of Epictetus, a Greek philosopher:

"Tentative efforts lead to tentative outcomes, therefore, give yourself fully to your endeavors. Decide to construct your character through excellent action and determine to pay the price of a worthy goal. The trials you encounter will introduce you to your strengths. Remain steadfast and one day you will build something that endures, something worthy of your potential."

As an ACTOR you will use your talent, ability and unlimited potential to take charge of your life. The first step is to take a few minutes to write out an action plan.

Action Plan:

What can you do to become an ACTOR in your life?

_____

_____

Is there something you always wanted to do but had the perception you couldn't? Is there something you could change, and if you did, would it make you a better person?

_____

_____

_____

_____

Goal:

Action Required:

Goal:

Action Required:

*   *   *   *

CHAPTER 8

Motivational Nutrients for the ACTOR Soul — Stories, Quotes and Parables to Energize and Stimulate Your ACTOR Factor

What do you think about life? Do you consider it boring? How about work? Meaningless ... only for money? Do you value your relationships? The next question is, what is your investment in these opportunities? I have met people who are bored, unenthusiastic, unmotivated about their life and they seem to let everyone know it. Have you ever come across these kinds of people? I find them constantly looking for new jobs, new work environments that appreciate them, and more exciting personal relationships. We usually think of this (generally speaking) as "the grass is greener on the other side" way of thinking.

In reality, you are responsible for creating your own motivated lifestyle. Zig Ziglar, well-known motivational speaker, says people who want to know what motivation is (and isn't) often challenge him. He says, "There are those who say that when someone goes to a motivational session they get all charged up, but a week later they're back where they were before they attended the session. In short, motivation isn't permanent ... right?" Of course not, but neither is brushing your teeth ... it helps if you do it on a regular basis. It would be foolish to think that by attending a seminar, listening to a speaker or reading this book it would have a permanent affect on the rest of your life ... it will be up to you to generate the motivation on a daily basis with or without the assistance of others.

The intent of this chapter is to provide you with a collection of stories, parables and quotes to help you stay motivated with a positive attitude. We have collected some old stories, stories from people we have met, and some personal stories. Read one a day to keep you focused on how special and blessed you are. Yes, blessed, because no matter how bad you think you have it, there are 2,000,000 plus people around the world in worse shape than you are.

Kellogg Brothers

At the age of 46, Will Kellogg found working with his brother unmotivating. His brother was a doctor who worked with Will on a cereal for a special patient. They created the Corn Flake® and Will wanted his brother to mass-market their new discovery.

Well, Dr. Kellogg was not interested in this foolish idea. Will convinced his brother to sell him his half of the rights to the cereal. Will was energized by the new venture, allowing him to develop keen business ability, marketing genius and customer sensitivity. Will Kellogg was able to generate his own motivation because he believed in his idea. There is an old country song that says a man without a dream is like a car without an engine. Will's gasoline was marketing his Corn Flakes® for mass consumption. Of course, the rest of Will's story is known; he became one of the richest men in America. He followed his dream, his vision, if you will. Now we all may not have the good fortune to discover Corn Flakes®, but whatever your dream, go for it! Make the most of what you have.

Micah's Story

I was attempting to impress upon my grandson, Micah, that he should live his life beyond perceived limits. "When I was your age," I said, already seeing his eyes starting to roll, "we lived on a farm in South Jersey and we would go to the Farmers Market every Saturday. This one Saturday while we were at the Farmers Market, Billy Tindall left some chickens on the front porch of our house while we were gone. When we returned home the chickens had gotten out of their crate due to a broken latch. Dad told us to go and round up the chickens. It took us hours, but we managed to find fourteen chickens. Your grandfather was a little disturbed at Billy for leaving the chickens in that bad crate. The next day Billy came over, and I remember your grandfather telling him that he didn't think it was a good idea to leave the chickens on the porch unattended. He told him it took us hours to get the chickens, and we only rounded up fourteen. Billy smiled and said,

"Fourteen chickens isn't too bad; I only delivered six!" Micah looked puzzled, and I realized that since he was only six years old, he might not have understood my point. You should always know your audience. I went on to explain that I wanted him to live beyond any limitations that others may put on him. I told him about my friend Earl Kornbrekke, who I played softball with on my recent trip to New Zealand. Earl was 58 years old and one of the best players on the senior tour. He was excellent at hitting and could catch and throw exceptionally well for his age. The special thing about Earl is that he only had one arm, and he has played sports all his life. If he had listened to others who felt that you must have two arms to play ball, he would never have been able to enjoy this passion in his life. Just how much can we accomplish when we don't put preconceived limits on the outcome. Your potential can be restricted by self-imposed limits. There are people who live their lives and die without ever having their power released. Don't let this happen to you, Micah! Live your life as though you had no idea how little or how much you can accomplish. Live beyond other perceived limitations of your ability. Whatever challenges life throws at you, see how many chickens you can find!

Justin's Story

One Saturday morning my granddaughter Jordan and her brother Justin were over visiting. I was in my office getting ready for a major presentation. Justin came in and said, "Grandpa, let's go out and play catch." I thought for a minute, almost saying I was too busy, but I remembered that song "The Cats in the Cradle" where the father never had time for his son, then the son grows up and becomes just like the father. Well, I had to think of something that was a win-win for both of us (or at least look like that). I told Justin I had a deal for him and if he helped Grandpa with the puzzle in the living room then I could go out and play catch with him. I said that Grandma had told me that I couldn't go out unless I put the puzzle together. I thought that was clever and would teach him several lessons. In addition, I knew this would give me hours to prepare for my presentation. Well, Justin agreed and went to work on the puzzle as soon as I left the room. I wasn't in my office more than 10 minutes when Justin came in and said, "Okay Grandpa, let's go play catch." I said, " Justin, I thought we had a deal." He replied, "We did." I said, "There's no way you put that puzzle together that quick." He replied, "Way!" I chuckled and proceeded to the living room. Sure enough, I was amazed at how accurately he assembled the puzzle. I said, "Justin, how in the world did you put that 150 piece puzzle together so fast?" He said, "Grandpa it was easy. On the other side of the puzzle are pictures of people, and when you put the people together, the world comes together." Here I am trying to teach some life lessons to my grandson and he's teaching me! We need to put the people in our lives together and our world will come together. It's all about relationships and interactions.

Jordan's Story

(As I stand I'm holding a large teddy bear). I guess you're wondering what I'm doing with this. Let me tell you the story behind it. It was a Saturday morning. I had just gotten up and had started getting my things together for a trip to California. In walks my granddaughter, Jordan, and starts with the questions:

"Grandpa, where are you going?"

"California" I answer

"Why?"

"For work."

"How long?"

"For a week."

"How long is that?"

"Five days."

"Is Grandma going with you?"

"No."

"Why not?"

"She has to work."

"Why?"

"So we can afford to pay the rent."

She didn't understand the humor, and I could see the next question by the look on her face. "Won't you be lonely without Grandma?" I said, "Yes, I will." Her face immediately showed great concern beyond her years. She then ran out of the room and returned shortly holding a brightly colored teddy bear. She said, "Grandpa, here, take my teddy bear and he will keep you company." I thought for a minute and said, "Sure, that will be great." She smiled as if now Grandpa would have a friend and left the room to tell Grandma what she had done. I put the little fellow on the bed and finished packing my bags.

After lunch I was ready to leave for the airport, and guess who was coming with me. That's right, little Jordan. We all got into the car and headed for the airport. I checked my bags with the porter and started saying my good-byes. As I turned to Jordan, I saw her holding the teddy bear. She said, "Grandpa, you almost forgot this." I said, "Gee, Jordan, thanks." Now picture this ... here is a 48-year-old man walking through the airport with his teddy bear (very bright and colorful). I think everybody was looking at me.

I finally got to my seat and sat down still holding the teddy bear. My attention immediately focused on the gentleman sitting in the next seat. He appeared very sad. I started a conversation and quickly came to find out that his wife had died just a few weeks before and he was going to visit his grandchildren. Immediately I shared with him why I was carrying the teddy bear. Without hesitation I asked if he wanted to hold the teddy bear. He laughed. I handed it to him and he took it and smiled. Do you know that his whole attitude changed and he sat there smiling and talking?

I'm not sure how far into the flight we were but I could hear a little boy a few rows behind me giving his mother a hard time. I didn't really like the way she was correcting his behavior ... it seemed a little cruel. He was about Jordan's age, so I decided to see if I could help. I got up and walked to his seat and asked the mother if there was anything I could do. She said, "No, he's just scared." I smiled and thought for a moment. I went back to my seat and asked the man if I could borrow the teddy bear. He smiled as if he knew what I was going to do. I asked the little boy if he would keep my teddy bear company. I explained it was his first flight and he was lonely and scared. He looks at me for a minute and said softly, "Yes" with a slight smile. Do you know, that the little boy was quiet the rest of the trip?

The boy returned the teddy bear as he got off the plane and said, "Take good care of him."

After having time to reflect on this trip, I realized that I had made a difference in those two people's lives with that teddy bear. Such a simple thing, but so powerful. It was then I realized that it's the small things we do that make a difference, both in people's lives and in our daily work. I started looking for small ways to make a difference in the way I live my life. I now understand what the following quote means: "We may never do great things, in fact, we don't have to because the little things we do can have great impact in life and happiness in others."

Remember, there is value in everything ... nothing is worthless ... even a watch that's broken is correct twice a day.

The Importance of Attitude — A Few Thoughts

"There is very little difference in people. But that little difference makes a big difference. The little difference is attitude. The big difference is whether it is positive or negative."
—W. Clement Stone

"It's not so much what happens to us, as what happens in us that counts, or what we think has happened to us."
—Tim Hansel

You have heard the saying "If you think you can ... or if you think you can't, you are right." Your attitude triggers your belief system, and what you believe has the power to create or destroy. I was at best an average English student and would have never thought it possible for me to write a book. I have three published books and it was because I had a vision and belief that I could do it, and I also had help from a network of friends. What is it that you want to do? Start today believing you can do it. Tomorrow, start working toward your belief and it will happen. Every dream needs a plan. Remember, if you fail to plan you are planning to fail.

Lou Holtz on Attitude: He believes that there is a strong relationship between ability and attitude. He believes, "Ability is what you are capable of doing. Motivation determines what you do. Attitude determines how well you do it."

So, to cultivate abilities, you need to maintain a healthy attitude. Focusing on the positive outcome will not only help you in sports, but life in general. Look for the positive action in everything you do. Just like the batter with a man on first base doesn't say to himself, "don't hit into a double play," they say, "hit it into the outfield." This is a positive way of looking at the situation. What you are actually doing is making a positive image in your mind of the outcome. This works in everything we do … and more than we think.

Enthusiasm: The word enthusiasm comes from the Greek root "en" and "these' and means, "God within". It is a fire … a passion within. Real enthusiasm is not something you "put on" and "take off" to fit the occasion. It's a way of life!

Little About Leadership … we are all leaders in some context:

"The ultimate responsibility of a leader is to facilitate other people's development as well as his own."
—Fred Pryor

"The leader's task, then, is to create an environment that is conducive to self-motivation."
—Nido Qubein

"As a manager, the important thing is not what happens when you are there but what happens when you are not there."
—Kenneth Blanchard & Robert Lorber

"To be a leader means willingness to risk and a willingness to love. Has the leader given you something from the heart?"
—Hubert H. Humphrey

"If people are coming to work excited ... if they're making mistakes freely and fearlessly ... if they're having fun ... if they're concentrating on doing things, rather than preparing reports and going to meetings — then somewhere you have a leader."
—Robert Townsend

"A business is a reflection of the leader. A fish doesn't stink just from the tail, and a company doesn't succeed or fail from the bottom."
—Gary Feldmar

"The world of the 90's and beyond will not belong to managers or those who make the numbers dance, as we used to say, or those who are conversant with all the business and jargon we use to sound smart. The world will belong to passionate, driven leaders — people who not only have an enormous amount of energy but who can energize those whom they lead."
—Jack Welch, Chairman & CEO of General Electric

"Perhaps more than anything else, leadership is about the 'creation of a new way of life.'"
—James M. Kouzes & Barry Z. Posner

Life's Little Hints for Success (many shared by the Dalai Lama)

1. Give people more than they expect, and do it cheerfully.

2. When you say, "I love you," mean it.

3. When you say, "I'm sorry," look the person in the eye.

4. Never laugh at anyone's dreams. People without dreams are like cars without any gasoline.

5. Love like you have never been hurt before.

6. In disagreements fight fairly — no name-calling.

7. Don't judge people by their relatives or by the life they were born into.

8. Take into account that great love and great achievements involve great risk.

9. Call your mother.

10. Say, "Bless you" when you hear someone sneeze.

11. Dance like there is no one watching.

12. When you lose, don't lose the lesson.

13. Follow the three R's: Respect for self, Respect for others, and Responsibility for all your actions.

14. Don't let a little dispute injure a great friendship.

15. When you realize you've made a mistake, take immediate steps to correct it.

16. Admit when you are wrong.

17. Smile when picking up the phone. The caller will hear it in your voice.

18. Don't be afraid to say, "You could be right."

19. Marry a person you love to talk to. As you get older, his/her conversational skills will become even more important.

20. Open your arms to change, but don't let go of your values.

21. Remember that silence is sometimes the best answer.

22. Live a good, honorable life. Then, when you get older and think back, you'll be able to enjoy it a second time.

23. In disagreements with loved ones, deal only with the current situation. Don't bring up the past.

24. Don't just listen to what someone is saying … listen to why they are saying it. Listen for the meaning behind the words.

25. Share your knowledge … it's a way to achieve immortality.

26. Never interrupt when you are being flattered.

27. Only be concerned with your business … mind your own business.

28. If you make a lot of money, put it to use helping others while you are living. It is wealth's greatest satisfaction.

29. Remember that not getting what you want is sometimes a wonderful stroke of luck.

30. Learn the rules so you know how to break them properly.

31. Judge your success by what you had to give up in order to get it.

32. Live with the knowledge that your character is your destiny.

Anyway

People are often unreasonable,

Illogical, and self-centered;

Forgive them anyway.

If you are kind,

People may accuse you of selfish, ulterior motives;

Be kind anyway.

If you are successful,

You will win some false friends and some true enemies,

Succeed anyway.

If you are honest and frank,

People may cheat you,

Be honest and frank anyway.

What you spend years building,

Someone could destroy overnight,

Build anyway.

If you find serenity and happiness,

They may be jealous,

Be happy anyway.

The good you do today,

People will often forget tomorrow,

Do well anyway.

Give the world the best you have,

And it may never be enough,

Give the world the best you've got anyway.

You see, in the final analysis,

It is between you and God,

It never was between you and them anyway.

—Author unknown

Words of Wisdom

Many people will walk in and out of your life,

But only true friends will leave footprints in your heart.

To handle yourself, use your head,

To handle others, use your heart.

Anger is only one letter short of danger.

Great minds discuss ideas,

Average minds discuss events;

Small, minds discuss people.

God gives every bird its food, but he does not throw it into its nest.

He, who loses money, loses much,

He, who loses a friend, loses more,

He, who loses faith, loses all.

Beautiful young people are acts of nature,

But beautiful old people are works of art.

Learn from the mistakes of others. You can't live long enough to make them all yourself.

The tongue weighs practically nothing, but so few people can hold it.

I dreamed I had an interview with God

"Come in," God said. "So, you would like to interview me?"

"If you have the time," I said.

God smiled and said, "My time is eternity and is enough to do everything; what questions do you have in mind to ask me?"

"What surprises you most about humankind?"

God answered, "That they get bored of being children, are in a rush to grow up, and then long to be children again.

That they lose their health to make money and then lose their money to restore their health.

That by thinking anxiously about the future, they forget the present, such that they live neither for the present nor the future. That they live as if they will never die, and they die as if they had never lived."

God's hands took mine and we were silent for a while and then I asked, "As a parent, what are some of life's lessons you want your children to learn?"

God replied with a smile, "To learn that they cannot make anyone love them. What they can do is to let themselves be loved. To learn that what is most valuable is not what they have in their lives, but who they have in their lives.

To learn that it is not good to compare themselves to others. All will be judged individually on their own merits, not as a group on a comparison basis!

To learn that a rich person is not the one who has the most, but is one who needs the least.

To learn that it only takes a few seconds to open profound wounds in persons we love, and that it takes many years to heal them.

To learn to forgive by practicing forgiveness.

To learn that there are persons who love them dearly, but simply do not know how to express or show their feelings.

To learn that money can buy everything but happiness.

To learn that two people can look at the same thing and see it totally different.

To learn that a true friend is someone who knows everything about them and likes them anyway.

To learn that it is not always enough that they be forgiven by others, but that they have to forgive themselves."

I sat there for a while enjoying the moment. I thanked him for his time and for all that he has done for me and my family, and he replied, "Anytime. I'm here 24 hours a day. All you have to do is ask for me, and I'll answer."

People will forget what you said,

People will forget what you did, but

People will never forget how you made them feel.

Daily Food for Thought

When things don't appear they are going your way, take a look at these, Instructions for Life:

- Remember that not getting what you want is sometimes a wonderful stroke of luck.

- Learn the rules so you know how to break them properly.

- Spend some time alone every day.

- Be gentle with the earth.

- Once a year, go someplace you've never been before.

- Approach love and cooking with reckless abandon.

- Too many people put off something that brings them joy just because they haven't thought about it, don't have it on their schedule, didn't know it was coming or are too rigid to depart from their routine.

- Have you ever thought the people that were worrying about their diets on the Titanic? Who passed up dessert at dinner that fateful night in an effort to stay on their diet?

- Don't let your favorite television program interfere with communication opportunities with your children.

- Don't wait for all the conditions in your life to be perfect to visit those who you love.

- Remember life is short. We never know what tomorrow might bring.

- Remember life has a way of accelerating, as we get older. The days get shorter and the list of promises to ourselves gets longer. Live for today while planning for tomorrow.

- Don't wake up one morning and the only thing you have to show for your life is a litany of "I'm going to," "I plan on" and "Someday, when things are settled down a bit" and "One of these days". Ah yes … one of these days.

- Do something you WANT to do … not something on your SHOULD DO list.

- I've learned … that the best classroom in the world is at the feet of an elderly person.

- I've learned … that when you're in love, it shows.

- I've learned … that just one person saying to me, "You've made my day!" makes my day.

- I've learned … that having a child fall asleep in your arms is one of the most peaceful feelings in the world.

- I've learned … that being kind is more important than being right.

- I've learned … that I can always pray for someone when I don't have the strength to help him in some other way.

- I've learned … that no matter how serious your life requires you to be, everyone needs a friend to act goofy with.

- I've learned … that sometimes all a person needs is a hand to hold and a heart to understand.

- I've learned ... that life is like a roll of toilet paper. The closer it gets to the end, the faster it goes.

- I've learned ... that money doesn't buy class.

- I've learned ... that it's those small daily happenings that make life so spectacular.

- I've learned ... that under everyone's hard shell is someone who wants to be appreciated and loved.

- I've learned ... that God didn't do it all in one day. What makes me think I can?

- I've learned ... that to ignore the facts does not change the facts.

- I've learned ... that when you plan to get even with someone, you are only letting that person continue to hurt you.

- I've learned ... that love, not time, heals all wounds.

- I've learned ... that the easiest way for me to grow as a person is to surround myself with people smarter than I am.

- I've learned ... that everyone you meet deserves to be greeted with a smile.

- I've learned ... that life is tough, but I'm tougher.

- I've learned ... that opportunities are never lost; someone will take the ones you miss.

- I've learned ... that when you harbor bitterness, happiness will dock elsewhere.

- I've learned ... that one should keep his words both soft and tender, because tomorrow he may have to eat them.

- I've learned … that a smile is an inexpensive way to improve your looks.

- I've learned … that I can't choose how I feel, but can choose what I do about it.

- I've learned … that when your newly born grand-child holds your little finger in his little fist, that you're hooked for life.

- I've learned … that everyone wants to live on top of the mountain, but all the happiness and growth occurs while you're climbing it.

- I've learned … that it is best to give advice in only two circumstances; when it is requested and when it is a life-threatening situation.

- I've learned … that the less time I have to work with, the more things I get done.

- I've learned … Laughter is the sun that drives winter from the human face.

If a dog were your teacher:

When loved ones come home, always run to greet them.

Never pass up the opportunity to go for a joy ride.

Allow the experience of fresh air and the wind in your face to be pure ecstasy.

When it's in your best interest — practice obedience.

Let others know when they've invaded your territory.

Take naps and stretch before rising.

Run, romp, and play daily.

Thrive on attention and let people touch you.

Avoid biting when a simple growl will do.

On warm days, stop to lie on your back on the grass.

On hot days, drink lots of water and lay under a shady tree.

When you're happy, dance around and wag your entire body.

*No matter how often you're scolded, don't buy into the guilt
thing and pout ... run right back and make friends.*

Delight in the simple joy of a long walk.

*Eat with gusto and enthusiasm. Stop when you have had
enough.*

Be loyal.

Never pretend to be something you're not.

If what you want lies buried, dig until you find it.

*When someone is having a bad day, be silent, sit close by and
nuzzle them gently.*

—Author Unknown

Great truths about life that little children have learned:

- No matter how hard you try, you can't baptize cats.

- When your Mom is mad at your Dad, don't let her
  brush your hair.

- If your sister hits you, don't hit her back. They
  always catch the second person.

- Never ask your 3-year old brother to hold a tomato.

- You can't trust dogs to watch your food.

- Reading what people write on desks can teach you a lot.
- Don't sneeze when someone is cutting your hair.
- Puppies still have bad breath, even after eating a *Tic Tac*.
- Never hold a *Dust Buster* and a cat at the same time.
- School lunches stick to the wall.
- You can't hide a piece of broccoli in a glass of milk.
- Don't wear polka-dot underwear under white shorts.
- The best place to be when you're sad is Grandpa's lap.

Great truths about life that adults have learned:

- Raising teenagers is like nailing *Jell-O* to a tree.
- There is always a lot to be thankful for, if you take the time to look. For example, I'm sitting here thinking how nice it is that wrinkles don't hurt.
- One reason to smile is that every seven minutes of every day, someone in an aerobics class pulls a hamstring.
- Carsickness is the feeling you get when the monthly payment is due.
- The best way to keep kids at home is to make a pleasant atmosphere and let the air out of their tires.
- Families are like fudge ... mostly sweet, with a few nuts.

- Today's mighty oak is just yesterday's nut that held its ground.

- Laughing helps ... it's like jogging on the inside.

- Middle age is when you choose your cereal for the fiber, not the toy.

- My mind not only wanders; sometimes it leaves completely.

- If you can remain calm, you just don't have all the facts.

Great truths about growing old:

- Growing old is mandatory; growing up is optional.

- Insanity is my only means of relaxation.

- Forget the health food. I need all the preservatives I can get.

Five Great Lessons: The Important Things Life Teaches You ...

Most Important Question

During my second month of nursing school, our professor gave us a pop quiz. I was a conscientious student and had breezed through the questions, until I read the last one: "What is the first name of the woman who cleans the school?" Surely this was some kind of joke. I had seen the cleaning woman several times. She was tall, dark-haired and in her 50's, but how would I know her name? I handed in my paper, leaving the last question blank. Before class ended, one student asked if the last question would count toward our quiz grade. "Absolutely," said the professor. "In your careers you will meet many people. All are significant. They deserve your attention and care, even if all you do is smile and say "Hello". I've never forgotten that lesson. I also learned her name as Dorothy.

Pickup in the Rain

One night, at 11:30 pm, an older African American woman was standing on the side of an Alabama highway trying to endure a lashing rainstorm. Her car had broken down and she desperately needed a ride. Soaking wet, she decided to flag down the next car. A young white man stopped to help her — generally unheard of in those conflict-filled 1960's. The man took her to safety, helped her get assistance and put her into a taxicab. She seemed to be in a big hurry! She wrote down his address, thanked him and drove away. Seven days when by and a knock came on the man's door. To his surprise, a giant console color TV was delivered to his home. A special note was attached. It read:

> *"Thank you so much for assisting me on the highway the other night. The rain drenched not only my clothes but also my spirits. Then you came along. Because of you, I was able to make it to my dying husband's bedside just before he passed away. God bless you for helping me and unselfishly serving others."*
>
> *Sincerely,*
>
> *Mrs. Nat King Cole*

Always Remember Those Who Serve

In the days when an ice cream sundae cost much less, a 10-year-old boy entered a hotel coffee shop and sat at a table. A waitress put a glass of water in front of him. "How much is an ice cream sundae?" "Fifty cents," replied the waitress. The little boy pulled his hand out of his pocket and studied a number of coins in it. "How much is a dish of plain ice cream?" he inquired. Some people were now waiting for a table and the waitress was a bit impatient. "Thirty-five cents," she said brusquely. The little boy again counted the coins. "I'll have the plain ice cream," he said. The waitress brought the ice cream, put the bill on the table and walked away. The boy finished the ice cream, paid the cashier and departed. When the waitress came back, she began wiping down the table and then swallowed hard at what she saw. There, placed neatly beside the empty dish, were two nickels and five pennies - her tip.

The Obstacle in Our Path

In ancient times, a king had a boulder placed on a roadway. Then he hid himself and watched to see if anyone would remove the huge rock. Some of the king's wealthiest merchants and courtiers came by and simply walked around it. Many loudly blamed the king for not keeping the roads clear, but none did anything about getting the big stone out of the way. Then a peasant came along carrying a load of vegetables. On approaching the boulder, the peasant laid down his burden and tried to move the stone to the side of the road. After much pushing and straining, he finally succeeded. As the peasant picked up his load of vegetables, he noticed a purse lying in the road where the boulder had been. The purse contained many gold coins and a note from the king indicating that the gold was for the person who removed the boulder from the roadway. The peasant learned what many others never understand. Every obstacle presents an opportunity to improve one's condition.

Giving Blood

Many years ago, when I worked as a volunteer at Stanford Hospital, I got to know a little girl named Liz who was suffering from a rare and serious disease. Her only chance of recovery appeared to be a blood transfusion from her 5-year old brother, who had miraculously survived the same disease and had developed the antibodies needed to combat the illness. The doctor explained the situation to her little brother, and asked the boy if he would be willing to give his blood to his sister. I saw him hesitate for only a moment before taking a deep breath and saying, "Yes, I'll do it if it will save Liz." As the transfusion progressed, he lay in bed next to his sister. He looked up at the doctor and asked with a trembling voice, "Will I start to die right away?" Being young, the boy had misunderstood the doctor; he thought he was going to have to give his sister all of his blood.

New Beauty

A married couple was in a terrible accident where the woman's face was severely burned. The doctor told the husband that they couldn't graft any skin from her body because she was too skinny.

So the husband offered to donate some of his own skin. However, the only skin on his body that the doctor felt was suitable would have to come from his buttocks. The husband and wife agreed that they would tell no one about where the skin came from and requested that the doctor also honor their secret. After all, this was a very delicate matter.

After the surgery was completed, everyone was astounded at the woman's new beauty. She looked more beautiful than she had ever been before! All her friends and relatives just went on and on about her youthful beauty!

One day, she was alone with her husband, and she was overcome with emotion at his sacrifice. She said, "Dear, I just want to thank you for everything you did for me. There is no way I could ever repay you."

"My darling," he replied, "think nothing of it. I get all the thanks I need every time I see your mother kiss you on the cheek."

Philosophy for St. Patrick's Day

There are only two things to worry about: Either you are well or you are sick.

If you are well, then there is nothing to worry about.

But if you are sick, there are two things to worry about: Either you will get well or you will die. If you get well, then there is nothing to worry about.

But if you die, there are two things to worry about: Either you will go to heaven or you will go to hell. If you go to heaven, then you have nothing to worry about.

But if you go to hell, you'll be so busy shaking hands with all your friends that you won't have time to worry!

Have a Happy St. Patrick's Day, and if you drink beer, make sure it's green!

Grady Johnson's Philosophy of Life (a song by Kenny Rogers):

Love you neighbor as yourself,

Don't use money to measure your wealth,

Trust in God but lock your door,

Buy low and sell high,

And slow dance more.

A simple philosophy for living your life. The same can be said for becoming the ACTOR in your life … it may be simple but it's powerful!

Every day you get better or worst, it's your choice … to be the Actor in your life or to be acted upon!

Final words of wisdom for the ACTOR:

1. No one can ruin your day without YOUR permission.
2. ACTORs will be about as happy as they decide to be.
3. Others can stop you temporarily, but only you can do it permanently.
4. Whatever you are willing to put up with is exactly what you will have.
5. Success stops when you do.
6. If the ACTORs ship doesn't come in, they will go out and get it.
7. You will never "have it all together."

8. Life is a journey ... not a destination. Enjoy the trip!

9. The biggest lie on the planet: "When I get what I want, I will be happy."

10. The best way to escape a problem is to solve it.

11. ACTORs have learned that ultimately, "takers" lose and "givers" win.

12. ACTORs know life's precious moments don't have value unless they are shared.

13. ACTORs know if you don't start, it's certain you won't arrive.

14. ACTORs know that we often fear the thing we want the most.

15. The ACTOR who laughs ... lasts.

16. ACTORs know that yesterday is in the past, tomorrow is in the future, and today is a present, so enjoy it!

17. ACTORs look for opportunities ... not guarantees.

18. ACTORs know life is what's coming ... not what was.

19. ACTORs realize that success is getting up one more time.

20. ACTORs understand what is "is."

21. When things go wrong, ACTORs don't go with them.

22. ACTORs view life like a cafeteria. They know if they
want something they have to get up and get it — it
won't be free and no one will bring it to them.

Beat That Clock (Lance Armstrong)

He couldn't hit a baseball. He couldn't catch a football. He couldn't shoot a basketball. But the young Lance Armstrong was determined to succeed in some sport.

"I was determined to find something I could succeed at. When I was in fifth grade, my elementary school held a distance-running race. I told my mother the night before the race, "I'm going to be a champ." She just looked at me, and then she went into her things and dug out a 1972 silver dollar. "This is a good luck coin," she said. "Now remember, all you have to do is beat that clock. I won the race."*

Winner of 1999 and 2000's Tour de France, Lance Armstrong has found success in the great sport of cycling. His specialty ... the time trial. Just Lance against the clock.

———————————

*Lance Armstrong with Sally Jenkins, *It's Not About the Bike* (New York: Putnam's 2000) p. 22-23.

Yesterday ... Tomorrow ... Today

There are two days in every week that we should not worry about. Two days that should be kept free from fear and apprehension.

One is yesterday ... with its mistakes and cares, its faults and blunders, its aches and pains. Yesterday has passed — forever beyond our control. All the money in the world cannot bring back yesterday. We cannot undo a single act we performed, nor can we erase a single word we've said ... Yesterday is gone!

The other day we should not worry about is tomorrow, with its impossible adversaries, its burden, its hopeful promise and poor performance. Tomorrow is beyond our control. Tomorrow's sun will rise either in splendor or behind a bank of clouds — but it will rise. And when it does, we have no stake in tomorrow, for it is yet unborn.

This leaves only one day — today. Any person can fight the battles of just one day. It is only when we add the burdens of yesterday and tomorrow that we break down. It is not the experience of today that drives people mad — it is the remorse for something that happened yesterday and the dread of what tomorrow might bring.

Let us therefore live one day at a time.

Rob Bryant Messages

Overcoming Spiritual Paralysis: I describe paralysis as being a lack of communication. Mine is obvious and is the lack of communication between my brain and legs. Unlike my paralysis, which happened in an instant, spiritual paralysis happens slowly from a lack of communication between us and God. It happens just one spiritual nerve at a time. Each time we say "no" to God, a few more nerves are cut until we are totally paralyzed. We can't feel or move and we are stopped spiritually. The cure comes when we begin or renew our relationship with God through Jesus Christ.

The Miracle Walk: This involves my struggle to walk again after a 55' fall from an oil rig. My back was broken and spinal cord severed. I was told that I would never walk again. I had no movement from the waist down, had several back operations, and serious sores and burns on my feet and legs. Yet through prayer and a miracle of God, enough movement returned for me to walk out of the largest rehabilitation center on the West Coast. Incredibly enough, after a year of training, I then went on to walk from Fort Worth to Dallas, using braces and crutches, setting a World Record.

The Row Across America: My trip (3,280 miles) began in Los Angeles, on April 2, 1990 on a Row-Cycle (three-wheeled-row machine). It concluded on the steps of the Capitol in Washington, DC on July 30. The reason for the trip was to encourage God's people that they don't have to give up in the face of adversity. Adventures of the trip included: 1200 miles of desert; the Southern Rockies; sixty M.P.H. head winds, heavy rains, hail; second degree burns on my feet; desertion; sickness (dangerous kidney infection); a crash in Wheeling, W.V., causing a concussion, broken toe, abrasions, and a deep puncture in my leg; and the Appalachian mountains. At the conclusion, the flag was flown over the Capitol in my honor and I received a Guinness World Record and two congressional records. I also received a letter from the President and an award from Arnold Schwarzenegger (Presidents Council on Physical Fitness). I typically share this on Sunday night to a packed auditorium.

There's Always One More Hill: This concerns rolling a wheel chair to the top of Enchanted Rock near Austin. I am the only paraplegic to ever do this. The question is: should we camp at the bottom of the hill, or do we utilize our talents and start climbing?

If all it takes to stop us is a hill; we are stopped. There is a time to wait on the Lord, but if it is a life style — we are spiritually paralyzed. I am not saying that we will always succeed. What appears to be failure in our eyes, may be success in God's eyes. Besides, by trying to be an example, our family and friends will be encouraged by our faith and courage!

Are You a Victor or a Victim? We can view our lives as a victim, and say that we have been treated unfairly. We can see wealthier, smarter, or stronger people and feel cheated. If that is our view of life, then we are victims, and may never accomplish the goals God has for our lives. On the other hand, we can see life as a victor. If we use our God given abilities and talents; we will be victors. The smallest one among us can slay the greatest giant, with the right attitude. We will all suffer in life just as Christ did, but can still have the ultimate victory.

I'll Climb the Mountain for You Dad! After watching me attempt to repel and rock climb at a camp in Colorado, my oldest son was the fastest youth his age at camp to climb from 8,000 feet to 12,000 feet. When I asked him how he managed to be the first to the top, he responded, "Dad, since you couldn't climb to the top, I climbed it for you. I was the fastest because when I do something for you, I want to do my best." This caused me to realize that when we do something for God, we need to do our best since we are living our lives for Christ. Our children need examples in order to achieve the goals God has for them.

The Race: In my youth, I was a very fast runner. Soon after my injury, I remembered a foot race between my father and I. Beating my father at the race was paramount in my youth, and I looked forward to sharing that moment with my sons. I realized that as a paraplegic I would never race with my children. This thought was overwhelming until I head God's voice say, "Rob, run the Race." I came to understand that if we make Jesus the goal line of our day, week, month, year, and life, we will cross finish lines greater than our wildest imagination. With this attitude, I've crossed two finish lines (both world records) and have many more ahead.

Follow Me: Lynn, a healthy young boy in my church used to play "follow me" with his dad. This was a follow-the-leader type game. By the time Lynn was twelve, muscular dystrophy left him in a wheelchair. The game of follow me then had to be played using wheelchairs and braces. On Lynn's deathbed, he told his father that he was leaving to see Jesus, and to follow him. Just like Lynn, we need to live in such a way that causes others to follow us toward Jesus. Whether we like it or not, our families are following our example. This message will leave a lasting impression on each family (especially the fathers).

Health Matters: I discuss health through diet, exercise, and inexpensive supplements which together lead to strength, weight loss, lower cholesterol levels, more energy, healthier heart, reduction of cancer risk, and feeling better about oneself.

What Matters Most?

The following is a brief reminder of what matters most in life. Just something to make us stop and think.

Take this quiz:

1. Name the five wealthiest people in the world.

2. Name the last five Heisman trophy winners.

3. Name the last five winners of the Miss America contest.

4. Name ten people who have won the Nobel or Pulitzer Prize.

5. Name the last six Academy Award winners for best actor.

6. Name the last decade's worth of World Series winners.

How did you do?

The point is, none of us remember the headliners of yesterday. These are no second-rate achievers. They are the best in their fields. But the applause dies. Awards tarnish. Achievements are forgotten. Accolades and certificates are buried with their owners.

Here's another quiz. See how you do on this one:

1. List two teachers who aided your journey through school.

2. Name three friends who have helped you through a difficulty.

3. Name five people who have taught you something worthwhile.

4. Think of three people who have made you feel appreciated and special.

5. Think of five people you enjoy spending time with.

6. Name half a dozen heroes whose stories have inspired you.

Easier? The lesson?

The people who make a difference in your life are not the ones with the most credentials, the most money, or the most awards. They are the ones that care. Pass this on to those people who have made a difference in your life (I just did!)

What I have learned

I have learned that, no matter what happens, how bad it seems today, life does go on, and it will be better tomorrow.

I've learned that you can tell a lot about a person by the way he/she handles four things: a rainy day, the elderly, lost luggage, and tangled Christmas lights.

I've learned that regardless of your relationship with your parents, you'll miss them when they're gone from your life.

I've learned that making a "living" is not the same thing as making a "life".

I've learned that life sometimes gives you a second chance.

I've learned that you shouldn't go through life with a catcher's mitt on both hands. You need to be able to throw something back.

I've learned that if you pursue happiness, it will elude you. But if you focus on your family, your friends, the needs of others, your work and doing the very best you can, happiness will find you.

I've learned that whenever I decide something with an open heart, I usually make the right decision.

I've learned that even when I have pains, I don't have to be one.

I've learned that every day, you should reach out and touch someone.

People love that human touch — holding hands, a warm hug, or just a friendly pat on the back.

I've learned that I still have a lot to learn!

Now I hope you have leaned something form these point to share with your friends.

If you would like to share your thoughts or stories with the author, please send them to:

ACTOR, P.O. Box 410893, Melbourne Florida 32941

THREE THINGS TO REMEMBER

Three things that can never come back:
1. Time
2. Words
3. Opportunity

Three things in life that can destroy a person:
1. Anger
2. Pride
3. Unforgiveness

Three things in life that you should never lose:
1. Hope
2. Peace
3. Honesty

Three things in life that are most valuable:
1. Love
2. Family & Friends
3. Kindness

Three things in life that are never certain:
1. Fortune
2. Success
3. Dreams

Three things that make a person:
1. Commitment
2. Sincerity
3. Hard work

MAYONNAISE JAR AND 2 CUPS OF COFFEE

When things in your life seem almost too much to handle, when 24 hours in a day are not enough —- remember the mayonnaise jar and the 2 cups of coffee.

A professor stood before his philosophy class and had some items in front of him. When the class began, he wordlessly picked up a very large and empty mayonnaise jar and proceeded to fill it with golf balls. He then asked the students if the jar was full. They agreed that it was.

The professor then picked up a box of pebbles and poured them into the jar. He shook the jar lightly. The pebbles rolled into the open areas between the golf balls. He then asked the students again if the jar was full. They agreed it was.

The professor next picked up a box of sand and poured it into the jar. Of course, the sand filled up everything else. He asked once more if the jar was full. The students responded with a unanimous "yes."

The professor then produced two cups of coffee from under the table and poured the entire contents into the jar effectively filling the empty space between the sand. The students laughed.

"Now," said the professor as the laughter subsided, "I want you to recognize that this jar represents your life. The golf balls are the important things—- your family, your health, your friends and your favorite passions—-and if everything else was lost and only they remained, your life would still be full.

The pebbles are the other things that matter like your job, your home and your car.

The sand is everything else — the small stuff. "If you put the sand into the jar first," he continued, "there is no room for the pebbles or the golf balls. The same goes for life. If you spend all your time and energy on the small stuff you will never have room for the things that are important to you.

"Pay attention to the things that are critical to your happiness. Play with your children. Spend time with your parents. Visit with grandparents. Take time to get medical checkups. Take your spouse out to dinner. Play another 18. There will always be time to clean the house and fix the disposal. Take care of the golf balls first—-the things that really matter. Set your priorities. The rest is just sand."

One of the students raised her hand and inquired what the coffee represented. The professor smiled saying, "I'm glad you asked."

It just goes to show you that no matter how full your life may seem; there's always room for a couple of cups of coffee with a friend."

IS there anyone in your life you should make time for before that little DASH is gone?

LEADERSHIP

Leadership in the 90's is the productive integration of diversity.
—**David Bruno**

Of those to whom much is given, much is required.
—**John F. Kennedy**

Give a man a fish and you feed him for a day. Teach a man to fish and you feed him for a lifetime.
—**Chinese Proverb**

Never tell people how to do things. Tell them what to do and they will surprise you with their ingenuity.
—**George Patton**

A leader is anyone who has two characteristics; first, he is going someplace; second, he is able to persuade other people to go with him.
—**W.H. Cowley**

Deep within man dwell those slumbering powers: powers that would astonish him, that he never dreamed of possessing; forces that would revolutionize his life if aroused and put into action.
—**Orison Swett Marden**

A hundred times a day I remind myself that my inner and outer life are based on the labors of other men, living and dead, and that I must exert myself in order to give in the same measure as I have received.
—**Albert Einstein**

*If we take people as we find them we may make them worse.
But, if we treat them as though they are what they should be,
we help them to become what they are capable of becoming.*
—Johann Wolfgang von Goethe

CREATING DESTINY

*We become what we think about. Life is a self-fulfilling
prophecy.*

*Life can only be understood backwards, but it must be lived
frontwards.*
—Kierkegaard

Concentrate on where you want to go, not on what you fear.
—Anthony Robbins

*Always think of what you have to do as easy and it
will become so.*
—Emile Coué

*To love what you do and can feel that it matters — how could
anything be more fun?*
—Katherine Jackson

*The greatest thing in the world is not so much where we stand
as in which direction we are moving.*
—Oliver Wendell Holmes

LEADERSHIP

Even eagles need a push:

The eagle gently coaxed her offspring toward the edge of the nest. Her heart quivered with conflicting emotions as she felt their resistance to her persistent nudging. "Why does the thrill of soaring have to begin with the fear of falling?" she thought. This ageless question was still unanswered for her.

Follow your dreams, for as you dream, so shall you become.

CREATING DESTINY

Vision is the art of seeing the invisible.
— Jonathan Swift

A moment's insight is sometimes worth a lifetime of experience.
—Ernest Holmes

Nothing in this world is so powerful as an idea whose time has come.
—Victor Hugo

Dream no small dreams for they have no power to move men.
—Johann Wolfgang von Goethe

The problems of the world cannot possibly be solved by skeptics or cynics whose horizons are limited by the obvious realities. We need men who can dream of things that never were.
—Oliver Wendell Holmes

PURPOSE

Our greatest need and most difficult accomplishment is to find the meaning in our lives.

To work at things you love, or for those you love, is to turn work into play and duty into privilege.
—Parlette

You have to do it yourself. No one else will do it for you. You must work out your own salvation
—Charles E. Popplestone

When skill and love work together, expect a masterpiece!

Visualize this thing you want. See it, feel it, believe in it. Make your mental blue print, and begin to build.
—Robert Collier

Nothing splendid has ever been achieved except by those who dared believe that something inside of them was superior to circumstance.
—Bruce Barton

FOCUS

The whole thing about getting things done is to know what to leave undone.

When your desires are strong enough you will appear to possess superhuman powers to achieve.
—Napoleon Hill

Above all be of single aim: have a legitimate and useful
purpose, and devote yourself unreservedly to it.
—James Allen

Concentrate: put all your eggs in one basket and
watch that basket.
—Andrew Carnegie

I had learned from years of experience with men that when a
man desires a single thing so deeply that he is willing to stake
his entire future on a single turn of the wheel in order to get
it, he is sure to win.
—Thomas Edison

LEADERSHIP

The value of a smile:

It costs nothing but creates much.

It enriches those who receive it, without impoverishing those
who give.

It happens in a flash and the memory of it sometimes lasts forever.

None are so rich they can get along without it, and none so
poor but are richer for its benefits.

It creates happiness in the home, fosters goodwill in a business, and is the countersign of friends.

It is rest to the weary, daylight to the discouraged, sunshine to the sad, and nature's best antidote for trouble.

Yet it cannot be bought, begged, borrowed or stolen, for it is something that is no earthly good to anyone till it is given away.

And if in the hurly-burly bustle of today's business world, some of the people you meet should be too tired to give you a smile, may we ask you to leave one of yours?

For nobody needs a smile so much, as those who have none left to give.

GOALS

Aim for success, not perfection. Never give up your right to be wrong, because then you will lose the ability to learn new things and to move forward with your life.
—Dr. David Burns

You must have long-range goals to keep you from being frustrated by short-range failure.
—Charles Noble

Goals determine what you are going to be. Goals are dreams with a time limit.
—Julius Erving

The secret to productive goal setting is in establishing clearly defined goals, writing them down and then focusing on them several times a day with words, pictures and emotions as if we've already achieved them.
—Denis Waitley

STORY WITH A MORAL

A water bearer in India had two large pots, each hung on the ends of a pole, which he carried across his neck. One of the pots had a crack in it while the other pot was perfect and always delivered a full portion of water.

At the end of the long walk from the stream to the house, the cracked pot arrived only half full. For a full two years this went on daily, with the bearer delivering only one and a half pots full of water to his house.

Of course, the perfect pot was proud of its accomplishments, perfect for which it was made. But the poor cracked pot was ashamed of its own imperfection, and miserable that it was able to accomplish only half of what it had been made to do.

After 2 years of what it perceived to be a bitter failure, it spoke to the water bearer one day by the stream. "I am ashamed of myself, and I want to apologize to you. I have been able to deliver only half my load because this crack in my side causes water to leak out all the way back to your house. Because of my flaws, you have to do all of this work, and you don't get full value from your efforts," the pot said.

The bearer said to the pot, "Did you notice that there were flowers only on your side of the path, but not on the other pot's side? That's because I have always known about your flaw, and I planted flower seeds your side of the path, and every day while we walk back, you've watered them. For two years I have been able to pick these beautiful flowers to decorate the table. Without you being just the way you are, there would not be this beauty to grace the house."

Moral: Each of us has our own unique flaws. We're all cracked pots, but it's the cracks and flaws we each have that make our lives together so very interesting and rewarding. You've just got to take each person for what they are, and look for the good in them. Blessed are the flexible, for they shall not be bent out of shape.

THANK GOD FOR ALL OF MY CRACKPOT FRIENDS!

* * * *

The
ACTOR
Factor

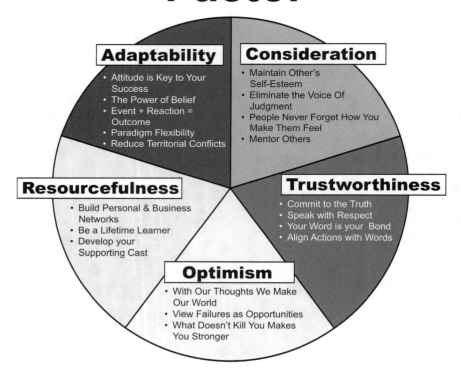

Adaptability
- Attitude is Key to Your Success
- The Power of Belief
- Event + Reaction = Outcome
- Paradigm Flexibility
- Reduce Territorial Conflicts

Consideration
- Maintain Other's Self-Esteem
- Eliminate the Voice Of Judgment
- People Never Forget How You Make Them Feel
- Mentor Others

Resourcefulness
- Build Personal & Business Networks
- Be a Lifetime Learner
- Develop your Supporting Cast

Trustworthiness
- Commit to the Truth
- Speak with Respect
- Your Word is your Bond
- Align Actions with Words

Optimism
- With Our Thoughts We Make Our World
- View Failures as Opportunities
- What Doesn't Kill You Makes You Stronger

Life Experience + The **ACTOR** Factor = Success

Leadership Qualities Survey

This **Leadership Qualities Survey** is designed to allow you to evaluate and rank the way you and your friends/family members/co-workers perceive your ACTOR qualities. Read the seven Quick Self-Check questions for each dimension and truthfully answer each question. At the bottom of each page, total your score for each dimension. When you have answered all the questions for each dimension, review the Leadership Qualities Scoring Sheet to see where you rank on each of the ACTOR qualities. Plot these points on the 'Self' ACTOR Assessment Graph, and follow the directions on the side of the page. The Reality Check portion of this survey allows friends/family members/co-workers to evaluate you on each of the ACTOR dimensions so you can see how others see these qualities in you. Have them answer the Reality Check questions and return the sheets to you for scoring. The Reality Check Scoring Sheet allows you to see where others rank your ACTOR qualities. Plot the points on the 'Other' ACTOR Assessment Graph and follow the directions on the side of the page. Compare the two graphs to see how you rank your ACTOR qualities and how others do. The ACTOR Reality Check Recap form allows you to compare multiple participants, such as team members.

ACTOR:

Adaptability

Consideration

Trustworthy

Optimistic

Resourceful

Adaptable - Quick Self-Check

Indicate below whether you agree or disagree with the statements by circling the number below your choice (Note: Read carefully because the scale changes)

	STRONGLY DISAGREE	DISAGREE	NEUTRAL	AGREE	STRONGLY AGREE
1 I embrace change - it is a welcome part of my world.	1	2	3	4	5
2 I believe I have little control over the impact of most changes.	5	4	3	2	1
3 I feel anxious when faced with managing major changes at work.	5	4	3	2	1
4 I enjoy challenging old ways of doing things.	1	2	3	4	5
5 I exhibit a positive attitude when confronted with major changes.	1	2	3	4	5
6 I feel threatened and overwhelmed by changes in my life.	5	4	3	2	1
7 I am good at developing new solutions to new and old problems.	1	2	3	4	5

TOTAL _____

Consideration - Quick Self-Check

Indicate below whether you agree or disagree with the statements by circling the number below your choice (Note: Read carefully because the scale changes)

	STRONGLY DISAGREE	DISAGREE	NEUTRAL	AGREE	STRONGLY AGREE
1 I consistently value the contributions of others by giving positive feedback/recognition.	1	2	3	4	5
2 I share information freely and often.	1	2	3	4	5
3 I "seek first to understand and then to be understood," even when others disagree with me.	1	2	3	4	5
4 I am good at "listening and responding with empathy."	1	2	3	4	5
5 I consistently maintain or enhance other's self esteem.	1	2	3	4	5
6 I value other's inputs in problem solving, even if they appear to be "way out there."	1	2	3	4	5
7 I look for new, creative, and unique ways to tailor rewards for employee successes.	1	2	3	4	5

TOTAL _____

Trustworthy - Quick Self-Check

Indicate below whether you agree or disagree with the statements by circling the number below your choice (Note: Read carefully because the scale changes)

		STRONGLY DISAGREE	DISAGREE	NEUTRAL	AGREE	STRONGLY AGREE
1	I am open and honest with my team members.	1	2	3	4	5
2	I show people I care about them.	1	2	3	4	5
3	I follow through on commitments in a timely manner.	1	2	3	4	5
4	Team members can count on my support.	1	2	3	4	5
5	I am open to positive and constructive feedback from my team members.	1	2	3	4	5
6	I give positive and constructive feedback to my team when it can help them develop.	1	2	3	4	5
7	I strive to create an environment that values open communication.	1	2	3	4	5

TOTAL _____

Optimistic - Quick Self-Check

Indicate below whether you agree or disagree with the statements by circling the number below your choice (Note: Read carefully because the scale changes)

	STRONGLY DISAGREE	DISAGREE	NEUTRAL	AGREE	STRONGLY AGREE
1 I take time to "envision the future" by periodically setting time aside for long-term planning.	1	2	3	4	5
2 I am very upbeat which is obvious when someone asks me, "How are you today?"	1	2	3	4	5
3 I believe it is important to challenge existing paradigms in order to improve our business.	1	2	3	4	5
4 I feel optimistic about the company's future.	1	2	3	4	5
5 In reality, an individual like me can have very little impact in my organization.	5	4	3	2	1
6 I believe sometimes it's okay to take a step backwards so we can take two steps forward.	1	2	3	4	5
7 I see most problems as opportunities to improve the situation.	1	2	3	4	5

TOTAL _____

Resourceful - Quick Self-Check

Indicate below whether you agree or disagree with the statements by circling the number below your choice (Note: Read carefully because the scale changes)

	STRONGLY DISAGREE	DISAGREE	NEUTRAL	AGREE	STRONGLY AGREE
1 I am good at breaking down barriers to achieve goals.	1	2	3	4	5
2 I work to establish good working relations with people outside my area in order to serve our customers better.	1	2	3	4	5
3 If you want a job done right, you have to do it yourself.	5	4	3	2	1
4 My reaction to a new, untried idea is sometimes "that will never work here."	5	4	3	2	1
5 I go out of my way to obtain needed inputs and resources so my team can get the job done, even when resources are scarce.	1	2	3	4	5
6 I ask for help when I can.	1	2	3	4	5
7 I don't hesitate to recommend other resources when I may not have the technical or other expertise to solve the problem.	1	2	3	4	5

TOTAL _____

Leadership Qualities Scoring Sheet

Adaptable:

30-35	You perceive yourself as highly adaptable; a change master.
25-29	You perceive yourself as relatively adaptable; comfortable with change.
22-24	You perceive yourself as somewhat adaptable; may not have a high comfort level with change.
16-21	You perceive yourself as uncomfortable with change.
Below 15	You perceive yourself as quite uncomfortable with change.

Consideration:

30-35	You perceive yourself as highly considerate.
25-29	You perceive yourself as relatively considerate.
22-24	You perceive yourself as somewhat considerate; you may want to consider changes/improvements in this area.
16-21	You perceive yourself as relatively inconsiderate; consider changes/improvements in this area.
Below 15	You perceive yourself as not considerate; this area may impact your ability to inspire and lead your employees. Consider changes/improvements in this area.

Trustworthy:

30-35	You perceive yourself as highly trustworthy.
25-29	You perceive yourself as relatively trustworthy.
22-24	You perceive yourself as somewhat trustworthy; this area may benefit from some attention.
16-21	You perceive yourself as relatively untrustworthy; area for development.
Below 15	You perceive yourself as very untrustworthy; area for development.

Optimistic:

30-35	You perceive yourself as highly optimistic and proactive.
25-29	You perceive yourself as relatively optimistic and proactive.
22-24	You perceive yourself as somewhat optimistic; this area may impact your ability to inspire and lead your employees.
16-21	You perceive yourself as relatively pessimistic; this area may impact your ability to inspire and lead your employees.
Below 15	You perceive yourself as very pessimistic and reactive; this area may impact your ability to inspire and lead your employees.

Resourceful:

30-35	You perceive yourself as highly resourceful.
25-29	You perceive yourself as relatively resourceful.
22-24	You perceive yourself as somewhat resourceful; this area may benefit from some attention.
16-21	You perceive yourself as not being terribly resourceful; area for development.
Below 15	You perceive yourself as not very resourceful; area for development.

What are my strengths and weaknesses in this area:

What actions can I take to improve in this area? (KABS - Knowledge, Attitude, Behaviors, Skills):

ACTOR Assessment Graph

"SELF"

Instructions:

Plot the data points for each ACTOR Dimension. Interconnect the plot points to form a line graph. Average all totals and draw a horizontal line across the graph at the average value point for each input.

Example:

A=20, C=25 T=15, O=30, R=12, Average= 20.4

Concentrate on below-average dimensions!

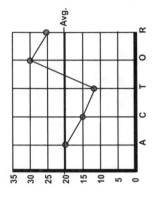

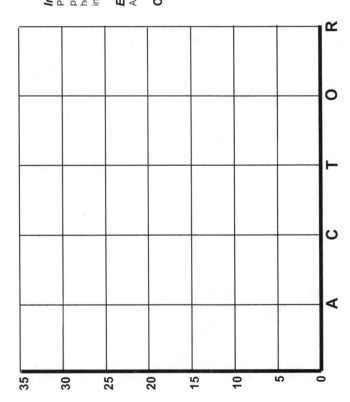

Reality Check
360 Degree Feedback

Person Receiving Feedback:

ACTOR:

Adaptability

Consideration

Trustworthy

Optimistic

Resourceful

Your open and honest feedback will be valued by the recipient.

Adaptable - Reality Check

Indicate below whether you agree or disagree with the statements by circling the number below your choice (Note: Read carefully because the scale changes)

	STRONGLY DISAGREE	DISAGREE	NEUTRAL	AGREE	STRONGLY AGREE
1 This person embraces change - it appears to be a welcome part of their world.	1	2	3	4	5
2 This person usually seems in control of changes in their life.	1	2	3	4	5
3 This person appears anxious when faced with managing major changes at work.	5	4	3	2	1
4 This person seems to enjoy challenging old ways of doing things.	1	2	3	4	5
5 This person generally exhibits a positive attitude when confronted with major changes.	1	2	3	4	5
6 This person appears to feel threatened and overwhelmed by changes in their life.	5	4	3	2	1
7 This person is always coming up with new solutions to new and old problems.	1	2	3	4	5

TOTAL _____

Please list a strength of this individual in this leadership quality: _____

Consideration - Reality Check

Indicate below whether you agree or disagree with the statements by circling the number below your choice (Note: Read carefully because the scale changes)

	STRONGLY DISAGREE	DISAGREE	NEUTRAL	AGREE	STRONGLY AGREE
1 This person consistently values the contributions of others by giving positive feedback/recognition.	1	2	3	4	5
2 This person shares info freely and often.	1	2	3	4	5
3 This person "seeks first to understand and then to be understood," even when others disagree with them.	1	2	3	4	5
4 This person is good at "listening and responding with empathy."	1	2	3	4	5
5 This person consistently maintains or enhances other's self esteem.	1	2	3	4	5
6 This person values other's inputs in problem solving, even if they appear to be "way out there."	1	2	3	4	5
7 This person looks for new, creative, and unique ways to recognize & reward employees for their successes.	1	2	3	4	5

TOTAL _____

Please list a strength of this individual in this leadership quality: _____

Trustworthy - Reality Check

Indicate below whether you agree or disagree with the statements by circling the number below your choice (Note: Read carefully because the scale changes)

		STRONGLY DISAGREE	DISAGREE	NEUTRAL	AGREE	STRONGLY AGREE
1	This person is very open and honest with all team members.	1	2	3	4	5
2	This person shows people they care about them.	1	2	3	4	5
3	This person follows through on commitments in a timely manner.	1	2	3	4	5
4	People can usually count on this person's support.	1	2	3	4	5
5	This person is open to positive and constructive feedback from others.	1	2	3	4	5
6	When giving feedback this person generally gives positive & constructive feedback to others when it can help them develop,	1	2	3	4	5
7	This person creates an environment that values open communication.	1	2	3	4	5

TOTAL _____

Please list a strength of this individual in this leadership quality: _____

Optimistic - Reality Check

Indicate below whether you agree or disagree with the statements by circling the number below your choice (Note: Read carefully because the scale changes)

	STRONGLY DISAGREE	DISAGREE	NEUTRAL	AGREE	STRONGLY AGREE
1 This person is good at "envisioning the future". This person develops long term plans that are communicated to others.	1	2	3	4	5
2 This person is very upbeat which is obvious even when you ask, "How are you today?"	1	2	3	4	5
3 This person believes it is important to challenge existing paradigms in order to improve the business.	1	2	3	4	5
4 This person always appears optimistic about the company's future.	1	2	3	4	5
5 This person gives the perception that an individual can have very little impact in their organization.	5	4	3	2	1
6 This person is willing to take a step backwards at times so they can take two steps forward.	1	2	3	4	5
7 This person sees problems as opportunities to improve the situation.	1	2	3	4	5

TOTAL _____

Please list a strength of this individual in this leadership quality: _____

Resourceful - Reality Check

Indicate below whether you agree or disagree with the statements by circling the number below your choice (Note: Read carefully because the scale changes)

	STRONGLY DISAGREE	DISAGREE	NEUTRAL	AGREE	STRONGLY AGREE
1	This person is good at breaking down barriers to achieve goals.	1	2	3	4	5
2	This person works to establish good working relations with people outside their area in order to serve our customers better.	1	2	3	4	5
3	This person does not delegate; they would rather do it themselves; they micromanage.	5	4	3	2	1
4	This person is not usually open to new, untried ideas. They prefer things that have worked right in the past.	5	4	3	2	1
5	This person will take whatever action necessary to obtain resources so their team can get the job done, even when resources are scarce.	1	2	3	4	5
6	This person doesn't usually ask for help from anyone.	5	4	3	2	1
7	This person doesn't hesitate to recommend other resources when they may not have the technical or other expertise to solve the problem.	1	2	3	4	5

TOTAL _____

Please list a strength of this individual in this leadership quality: _____

Reality Check

Leadership Qualities Scoring Sheet

Adaptable:

30-35 Others perceive you as highly adaptable; a change master.
25-29 Others perceive you as relatively adaptable; comfortable with change.
22-24 Others perceive you as somewhat adaptable; may not have a high comfort level with change.
16-21 Others perceive you as uncomfortable with change.
Below 15 Others perceive you as quite uncomfortable with change.

Consideration:

30-35 Others perceive you as highly considerate.
25-29 Others perceive you as relatively considerate.
22-24 Others perceive you as somewhat considerate; you may want to consider changes/improvements in this area.
16-21 Others perceive you as relatively inconsiderate; consider changes/improvements in this area.
Below 15 Others perceive you as not considerate; this area may impact your ability to inspire and lead your employees. Consider changes/improvements in this area.

Trustworthy:

30-35 Others perceive you as highly trustworthy.
25-29 Others perceive you as relatively trustworthy.
22-24 Others perceive you as somewhat trustworthy; this area may benefit from some attention.
16-21 Others perceive you as relatively untrustworthy; area for development.
Below 15 Others perceive you as very untrustworthy; area for development.

Optimistic:

30-35 Others perceive you as highly optimistic and proactive.
25-29 Others perceive you as relatively optimistic and proactive.
22-24 Others perceive you as somewhat optimistic; this area may impact your ability to inspire and lead your employees.
16-21 Others perceive you as relatively pessimistic; this area may impact your ability to inspire and lead your employees.
Below 15 Others perceive you as very pessimistic and reactive; this area may impact your ability to inspire and lead your employees.

Resourceful:

30-35 Others perceive you as highly resourceful.
25-29 Others perceive you as relatively resourceful.
22-24 Others perceive you as somewhat resourceful; this area may benefit from some attention.
16-21 Others perceive you as not being terribly resourceful; area for development.
Below 15 Others perceive you as not very resourceful; area for development.

Note: Most of us can recognize our weaknesses. Sometimes we don't notice our strengths because they are natural and we don't get told as much about them. Important to note, however, that sometimes an over-use of a strength can be a career limiting weakness.

What strengths do others perceive in you? (List)

ACTOR Assessment Graph

"OTHER"

Instructions:
Plot the data points for each ACTOR Dimension. Interconnect the plot points to form a line graph. Average all totals and draw a horizontal line across the graph at the average value point for each input.

Example:
A=20, C=25 T=15, O=30, R=12, Average= 20.4

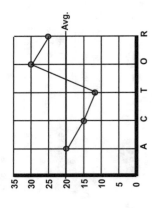

Concentrate on below-average dimensions!

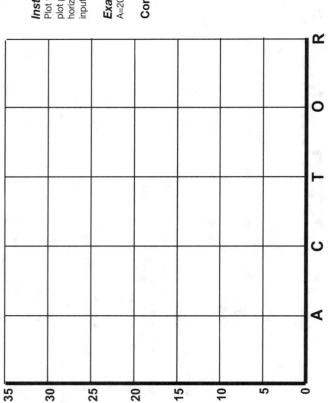

ACTOR – Reality Check

REALITY CHECK
Recap Page

Person	A	C	T	O	R
A					
B					
C					
D					
Total **Avg. (Round Up)**					
Strengths					

ANSWERS TO PARADIGM FLEXIBILITY QUESTIONS
ON PAGE 16

TASK: Move three and put two back
making the same design

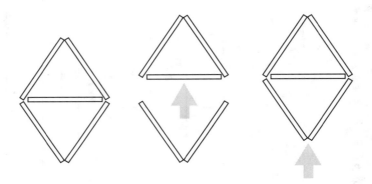

Answer: Move the three top matches upward, then move the two lower ones upwards to complete the diamond.

TASK: Make the following Roman numeral into the
number 6 using only one line:

IX

Answer: Write an 'S' in front of the IX to spell 'six'.

SIX